The MIND *of* CHINA

THE MIND OF CHINA

Ben-Ami Scharfstein

BASIC BOOKS, INC., PUBLISHERS
NEW YORK

© 1974 by Basic Books, Inc.
Library of Congress Catalog Card Number: 73-81198
SBN 465-04622-3
Manufactured in the United States of America
DESIGNED BY VINCENT TORRE
74 75 76 77 78   10 9 8 7 6 5 4 3 2 1

PREFACE

CHINA has undergone a great, enigmatic, and no doubt still unfinished revolution. Can this revolution be as radical as it seems? Is it possible for China to continue to live and its profound old culture to die all at once? Do the old ideals still in any way actuate the leaders of contemporary China, and if not them, at least their followers? Scholars debate the issue and a convincing answer cannot yet be given. But I can think of no instance in history of the sudden death of a tradition by which such enormous numbers of men have lived in so many related variations for so long a time. Everything I know leads me to think that whatever the changes in Chinese life, the memory of the past will not simply be obliterated or function only as the historic evil from which the Chinese have now been rescued. Old China will somehow continue to live in the bones of the new.

But even if the intellectual and artistic culture of old China dies the death which I think is hardly possible, it has been extraordinarily creative and it ought not to be forgotten by the world. It is too great a part of the human accomplishment in general. I have tried, therefore, to give a concentrated but not excessively superficial view of this culture and, to this end, to allow many of the old Chinese to speak, not only in my voice, but in their own as well. The first chapter, *Rulers and Sons*, furnishes a kind of political and sociological background for the succeeding chapters, on artists, historians, cosmographers, and philosophers.

I owe thanks to those who have helped me, first to the Sinologist, Professor Donald Leslie, who went over the text with me very carefully and helped me to correct errors and misleading statements. Mr. Joel Gower gave his expert photographic help with the illustrations. To the Am Oved Publishing Co., of Tel-Aviv, I am grateful for permission to use the material on the Chinese artist that appeared in my book, *The Artist in World Art*. Finally, my thanks go to all the scholars whose works I have used. Should I for some reason have failed to acknowledge my debt to any of them, I ask their pardon. Without them, there is nothing of value I could have said here. I have attempted to communicate with every publisher whose formal permission is required. Sometimes it was not clear to whom to turn, and I may, of course, have made inadvertent omissions. If this is the case, I shall be happy to make the normal amends.

Ben-Ami Scharfstein

CONTENTS

The MIND *of* CHINA

1

Rulers and Sons

THE EMPIRE OF
FILIAL PIETY

THE China of this book is the China of tradition, which appears to have died, perhaps forever, during the present century. The book therefore has a soberly magical aim, to enter into the consciousness that traditional Chinese art, literature, history, and philosophy have kept alive.

I have meant to be brief, and have omitted many things that are in themselves of great interest. I have hardly dealt with the early, formative philosophies of China, with Buddhism, or with the more popular literature—that is, the drama and novel. I have concentrated instead on a few subjects and a limited time, roughly the second millennium A.D. It is China of the second millennium which has left us the fullest and most dependable evidence, which contains the earlier Chinas embedded within itself, and which still confronts us in traditionally educated Chinese.

The attempt I am making here raises a difficult but unavoidable question. Does it make even metaphorical sense to consider China to have had a single mind? China is not obviously an individual. It is geographically heterogeneous. Its inhabitants are of different ethnic origins, and its languages, although Chinese, are as different from one another as the Latin languages, French and Italian, for example. Besides, China has for centuries been a heavily populated country. In 1393 it already had 60 million inhabitants, in 1600, 150 million, and in 1800, 300 million. These tens and then hundreds of millions, scattered on mountains and arid plains and crowded into river valleys and along coastlines, filled every possible occupation and every rung on the ladder of wealth, power, learning, skill,

3

and sensibility. What, then, can it mean to speak of "the mind of China"?

The nature of our sources makes the answer simpler than it might otherwise be. Chinese thought has been transmitted by a class of literate men with an almost uniform education. The mind of China was created or at least expressed by them, and not by the illiterate majority. The implication is not, of course, that literate Chinese have been intellectually identical. But if their culture has had any unity, has been more than a mere succession of events, it must have had some approximately stable characteristics. Historians used to say that China was the very model of a static nation, so unchanging that it had, so to speak, gone out of history. Most of the more specialized historians now maintain the opposite. These specialists are right, I think, and I therefore do not believe that the stable characteristics of the Chinese have been more basic to their culture than the unstable ones. Nevertheless, it is the former that have made Chinese thought coherently Chinese and arguably single.

The notion of a general mind is itself characteristically Chinese. Confucius once told a disciple that there was one thread that ran through his doctrine. He was later taken to have meant that human beings share in a single mind, which penetrates into all things like blood into the body. But the mind of the Chinese is different from ours, and Chinese scholars tend to deny that a Westerner can really grasp it. Whether or not they are exaggerating, it is clear that no single person, even a Chinese scholar, can grasp all of it. The notion of this mind is helpful—it is a thread of understanding that leads through the maze of facts; but the mind of China is neither exactly singular nor plural.

The Center:
Families and
Filial Piety

We may begin at the center from which all life radiated. The traditional Chinese felt, far more than we do, that the center of human existence was the family. Ideally, the family consisted of a number of generations living together in the same household. Because the Chinese believed that the spirits of their ancestors remained somehow active and understanding, the spirits were invited to all family occasions. Tablets commemorating ancestors were kept and honored in a special hall. It was supposed that the ancestral spirits, if pleased, would help the family, and, if seriously displeased, would cause it harm. The children yet unborn were also considered members of the family, which was morally obliged to hand its tradition and property on to them. (See Plate I.)

Throughout its history, China remained basically rural. The security of the family depended on the land it owned. To sell family land was like participating in a fraction of the family's death, and to buy land for the family was like holding a wedding, with its promise of fruitfulness and strength.

Apart from land, industriousness, and traditional decency, it was learning that gave a family its prestige. A family that had an advanced scholar would advertise its honor by setting a double flagpole up in front of its door. But even the most industrious, decent, and learned family might be scattered or destroyed by plague, flood, or famine.

The family protected its members. Yet the life of the individual was not easy. After a few carefree years, a child would feel the shock of an increasingly harsh discipline. The father was supposed to be, and often was, unbendingly severe, and his son, who had learned to feel ill at ease in his presence, had little to say to him that was not strictly necessary. The mother was the children's confidante, emotional support, and source of love. A Chinese proverb says, "One may give up a father even if he is a magistrate, but not a mother even if she is a beggar."

Marriages were arranged long in advance and celebrated at a relatively early age. The wife, who had to move to her husband's family, was forbidden to show public affection for him or to refer to him publicly except with an impersonal "he." Because she had to obey and serve her mother-in-law, her fate could be quite sad if she married into an unsympathetic family. Her husband might find himself torn between her and his jealous mother. The husband, too, had

5

to be careful not to show his affection openly. As time went on, however, the aging couple could relax in public and perhaps even allow themselves to be seen holding hands. If they moved away from the ancestral home, or if they outlived the senior members of their family, they would become family heads in their own right, and, wherever they were, their children would serve them respectfully as they had once served their own parents. Life was likely to be just to anyone, even a woman, who survived it long enough. Having paid the price of obedience, the survivor could relax into the comfortable dictatorship of Chinese patriarchs.

The Dominance
of Elders

Parents and children: sometimes all the morality of China seems concentrated in their relationship. The old literature of China is filled with exhortations to children, of every age, and to younger brothers. Confucius, the revered quasi-father of them all, asks rhetorically, "Are not filial devotion and respect for the elders in the family the very foundation of human-heartedness?"

The *Classic of Filial Piety*, which seems to have been written by a confirmed parent, goes further still and says:

Now filial piety is the root of all virtue, and that from which all teaching comes. . . . Our bodies, in every hair and bit of skin, are received by us from our parents, and we must not venture to injure or scar them. This is the beginning of filial piety. When we have established ourselves in the practice of the Way, so as to make our name famous in future ages and thereby glorify our parents, this is the goal of filial piety.

The *Book of Rites* has a curt, practical formula: "Filiality has three expressions: the greatest is to honor one's parents; the second is to refrain from disgracing them; the third is to support them." A Chinese proverb, not necessarily ancient, spells out the advantage of filial piety to parents: "Men plant trees because they want the shade; men rear sons to provide for old age." Another, as unhumorous as it is practical, adds: "Girls too are necessary!"

6

It should not be supposed that filial piety and the dominance of elders were left to exhortations, proverbs, and consciences. The law enforced them rigorously. As the recognized head of the family, the father or grandfather had almost unlimited authority over it. If he beat his adult son till the blood showed, he was within his rights, and the son was instructed "not to be angry but to be still more reverential and filial." A child, of whatever age, who scolded, cursed, beat, or seriously disobeyed his parents, could be put to death by them without fear of intervention by the law.* (See Plate II.)

Parents also could hand their children over to the authorities, who would beat or imprison those guilty of any of the following kinds of "unfilial behavior": legal prosecution of parents or grandparents; residence away from parents or grandparents; separation of one's property from that of parents or grandparents; failure to support parents or grandparents; marriage, entertainment, or other neglect of mourning for one's parents before the end of the required mourning period.

The dominance of the elders was emphasized by the law which defined as a crime the incitement of a parent or grandparent to suicide. This was the crime charged when a parent or grandparent committed suicide out of anger at a member of his family. It might be charged even when the death of a parent was accidental, as is shown by the following two cases taken from the legal records of the last, Ch'ing Dynasty:

Ch'en Wen-hsuan scolded his son when the latter brought him a cup of cold tea. The father poured the tea on the ground and picked up a stick with which to beat his son. The son ran away, the father after him. The ground was slippery because of the spilled tea and Wen-hsuan lost his footing, struck his head, and died as a result of his injury.

The verdict in this case was "detention in prison for strangling."

* In contemporary China, says an investigator, "The denunciation of one's father is the symbolic act *par excellence*. Through it the intellectual is to cast off his tie to filialism entirely; after this let no man regard him as a traditional filial son" (R. Lifton, *Thought Reform and the Psychology of Totalism*, Baltimore, Penguin Books, 1967, p. 438).

In another case, however, the verdict was reduced, as the text explains:

Chiang Shao-hsien was beating his wife because she had not ground the grain. His mother was in her room and shouted to him to stop. The wife, however, was screaming so loudly that the son did not hear his mother. The mother then came out of her room, but stumbled and died from the fall. The governor of Kweichow convicted Shao-hsien of disobeying instructions and causing the mother to commit suicide. At the same time, however, he reported the facts to the Ministry of Justice, saying that Shao-hsien did not purposely offend his mother. The Ministry of Justice decided that as the mother's voice had not been heard the son had not disobeyed her instructions, and that furthermore the mother's stumbling was not expected, and that she did not mean to kill herself. The punishment was reduced to banishment with the emperor's consent.

When parents had such power in custom and law, their children were, of course, afraid of them and conformed to their wishes. Family quarrels were settled out of court as far as possible. Resort to judges was not only considered shameful, but was expensive and, considering the legal penalties, dangerous. At its extreme, the principle upheld by the courts was simply that the senior member of a family was always in the right. A sixteenth-century official said:

I have seen some officials who punished the guilty party when an elder and a younger man accused each other before the court. . . . When this kind of case occurs, even though the senior is absolutely wrong he should be tolerated and pardoned. Even if he speaks offensively to the official, punishment should not be meted out to him lest others think that the senior was punished because of the junior. This is the very essence of ethical principle.

Confucian Political Values and Indoctrination

According to the standard Chinese view, filial piety, brotherly respect, and the general dominance of elders were the principles not only of family life, but of political life as well.

8

As a classic sentence put it, "The efficient ruling of a state necessarily consists in bringing its families into an ordered harmony." A properly graduated respect on the side of a son or subject was supposed to be met by a properly graduated authority on the part of a parent, official, or ruler, respect teaching respect and kindness kindness. The harmonies of family and state, the Confucians said, were complementary and mutually contagious.

Literate Chinese absorbed these values with their training in general and their books in particular. Villagers, however, were unlikely to be well trained in the Confucian sense, and quite unlikely to be literate. The government searched for ways to indoctrinate them. In the mid-seventeenth century, it decided that local scholars or suitable elders should lecture on the Imperial Maxims and on the villagers' good and evil deeds. These Imperial Maxims were few, short, and telling:

1. Perform your filial duties to your parents.
2. Honor and respect your elders and superiors.
3. Maintain harmonious relations with your neighbors.
4. Instruct and discipline your sons and grandsons.
5. Let each work peacefully for his own livelihood.
6. Do not commit wrongful deeds.

Unfortunately, as the government discovered, even the shortest and most moral commandments do not always convert those who are forced to learn them by heart. It therefore decided to amplify the Imperial Maxims, in order to remove any shadow of doubt from their meaning in practice. It is unnecessary to repeat the full amplification, for that of the last Maxim, "Do not commit wrongful deeds," may serve as an example. Its meaning, amplified, was, first, that one should explain the laws to warn the ignorant or perverse; secondly, that one should put a stop to false accusations; thirdly, that one should refuse to conceal fugitives; fourthly, that one should pay taxes in full; fifthly, that neighbors should organize so as to make thievery difficult; and lastly, that one should settle cases of animosity in a peaceful way.

The lecture system was extended and soldiers, too, were exposed to it. The results are naturally hard to judge, but there is evidence that the lectures, although effective at times, were often an empty formality; and they led in the end to a new method of police surveillance. The villagers were too occupied with their own survival to care about their distant rulers. Their attitude is illustrated by a report of the Abbé Huc, a mid-eighteenth-century traveler in China. The Emperor having recently died, the Abbé asked a group of peasants what they thought about the imperial succession. The answer was that politics was the business of those who were paid for it, the scholar-officials. The peasant who acted as spokesman said, "Don't let us torment ourselves about what does not concern us. We should be great fools to want to do political business for nothing."

The Social Hierarchy

In the hierarchy of Chinese life, everyone was or was supposed to be somehow supported and supportive, served and serviceable, imperious and submissive, exactly in accord with his social class, subclass, and individual status. Of the social classes, three were recognized as the most important —that of the officials, most of whom had passed examinations to prove their scholarship; that of ordinary, legally respectable people, who may be called commoners; and that of socially contaminated or "mean" people. The Chinese distinguished between these classes and the subclasses within them with the greatest thoroughness. These distinctions were expressed not only in terms of titles, power, and salaries, but also by flags, hats, shoes, clothing, belts, ornaments, carriages, horses, and wives, as well as by houses, beds, mats, utensils, food, drink, sacrifices, and funerals.

Officials had legal privileges. The most important were exemption from corporal punishment, from the labor and head taxes, from the giving of testimony in commoners' cases, and from assault by commoners. They had other, more showy privileges as well. If we confine ourselves to the Ch'ing Dynasty (1644–1912), officials, unlike commoners, were allowed to have large houses, graduated according to their rank; official robes, according to rank; ornamental buttons on their hats, according to rank; expensive furs, according to rank; ornaments of so-called golden brass and of silver, gold, and jade; gold-decorated furniture and utensils; and sedan chairs, marked according to rank and accompanied by no more than the number of attendants allowed the passenger's rank. A few concessions were made to commoners, who were allowed to own a single piece of gold-decorated furniture, a single gold wine-cup, a single pair of gold earrings for the women, and a properly marked sedan chair for the old or ill. But the concessions never went so far as to allow them to have their house-beams painted in color. In spite of the penalties set by the law, however, violations of these rules seem to have been usual.

Among the commoners, the highest in status were the scholars, who were regarded as potential officials and granted some of the officials' esteem and privilege. Below them were the farmers, who were praised because they worked to support everyone else. Last were the artisans and merchants, who were looked down upon because, as convention had it, they were not really productive.

The "mean" people, somewhat differently classified in different places, included slaves, prostitutes, entertainers, and beggars; and also various types of government employees, such as messengers, jailers, coroners, policemen, and those who administered corporal punishment. "Mean" people were all barred by law from the government examinations, the only established path to a higher social status. If discovered applying for an examination, the member of a "mean" family would be given a hundred strokes of the bamboo. Intermarriage with commoners was forbidden by law, though no punishment was specified for a commoner who married a female slave or prostitute. Often the "mean" people could be identified by the clothing the law prescribed for them; and there were families that expelled members who turned actor, prostitute, or "mean" government employee.

The Villager
at School

In traditional China, book learning had very great prestige. From the standpoint of the government, it was important because it spread Confucian values among the people, indoctrinated the officials who were needed to govern China, and helped to assimilate able, ambitious men into the government apparatus. For the ambitious men themselves, and for their families, book learning was the key to position and power. And because China had long had a rich literature, books had attractions of their own. China was, therefore, a comparatively bookish nation. A Dominican missionary who lived in China during the middle of the seventeenth century wrote in appreciation:

> The Chinese Nation is much addicted to Learning and inclin'd to Reading. I have met Men on the Road in Sedans or Palankins on Mens Shoulders, with a Book in their Hands. In Cities I have often seen Mandarines in the same manner. The Tradesmen and Shopkeepers sit behind their Counters with Book before them. To encourage the Children to learn, in their Primmers they have particular Examples, and the Cuts of Men that rise to great Preferment by their Learning. Among the rest there is one of a Man that kept Cows; he rode upon one of them, as is usual in that Country, with a Book laid on her Horns that serv'd instead of a Desk, and so he studied all the Day. After some years he grew so learned, that he took his Degree, and came to be a great Mandarine.

Chinese elementary schools usually were set up by a teacher or a family or group of families. Reading and writing were taught by means of the Confucian Classics, which every advanced student had to know almost word for word. Study of the Classics took long years of mechanical memorizing under teachers who prodded their students with harsh punishments. Yet the importance of formal education was so widely recognized that there were schools even in the small villages.

What was Chinese village education like? How did the schoolboys themselves feel? We get a clue from an anthropologist whose childhood was spent in a Chinese village with a traditional school. He hated it and kept running away from it. After many beatings, he finally stayed in the classroom, but slept while the teacher was there and led the boys on a rampage when the teacher was out. He writes:

Most boys were not in the least interested in their schoolwork. The school itself was a one-room affair with a dirt floor. The walls were dark and the windows pasted over with grimy old paper so that the lighting was very bad. The tables, benches, and stools were brought by the pupils from their homes. Boys ranging in age from six to twenty years were herded together into one room. The students were sent to school before the sun was up in the morning, about an hour before the teacher arrived. Each boy was expected to use this time in reading his assignment at the top of his voice and to memorize what he was reading. . . . When the teacher appeared, another hour was spent in reviewing the textbooks. Then the boys were called upon to recite one by one. Each boy, as his turn came, placed his books on the teacher's desk, turned his back, and recited all or part of his assignment. All this took place before breakfast. Both pupils and teachers went home to eat. When they returned from the morning meal, they practiced calligraphy and tried their skill at filling in couplets and composing poems. Occasionally there were lectures on good manners and on the ethical doctrines of Confucius. The teacher gave out the new assignments to each pupil individually, as there was no class system. . . . The few boys who excelled and who were able to continue at school prepared for the Imperial Examination as soon as they finished the regular courses. They studied the poems and essays written by the early scholars and also wrote some of their own.

We have said before that most of the boys did not like the school. They learned their lessons by rote without understanding the meaning of what they were required to read. Except for the *Jih Yung Za Tze* [a dictionary of everyday words and terms], all the textbooks were completely incomprehensible to them, but they were compelled to read and to remember what they had read. It was painful work. Unfortunately, neither the teacher nor the boys' parents had any interest in remedying the situation, and the boys were forced into endless memorizing and were punished severely if they failed. . . .

The old-fashioned school offered no recreation. As a rule, a schoolboy had to sit on his seat and keep quiet all the time. When he heard the noise, the laughter, and the wild running of the boys out on the street, he and all the other pupils felt a great longing to join them, but did not dare. The only chance for fun was when the teacher was not in school. On these rare occasions the boys' energy, imagination, and joy broke forth immediately and simultaneously. They overturned tables and piled up benches as a stage for an impromptu "show." They threw paper balls and water holders in a game of "war." They stole into the vegetable garden near the schoolhouse to pick fruits, cucumbers, or radishes. The shouting, swearing and laughing could be heard even by distant neighbors. One or two small boys stood guard at a far corner to wait for the teacher's coming. As soon as he was sighted and the signal was given, all the boys ran wildly back into the schoolhouse and put everything in order. Occasionally they were discovered and punished. (See Plate III.)

The Prince at School

It is interesting to move to the other extreme of the social hierarchy and see how a prince was educated for his future role, that of Emperor. Consider, for example, Ch'ien-lung, who was born in 1711 and was Emperor from 1736 to 1795. He was trained to become both the gentlemanly scholar-esthete and the ruler, and his education was correspondingly severe, painstaking, and full. As a Chinese gentleman, he learned not only the Confucian Classics, but also to compose paintings, calligraphy, and poetry. As a potential soldier, he learned to ride, hunt, shoot, and take part in military planning. And as the future Emperor, he learned to play the central role in Court ceremonial and, in a word, to rule.

The values Ch'ien-lung was taught were essentially those taught any Chinese, beginning with the village schoolboy. His teachers were chosen to be sound rather than brilliant. He first learned the Confucian Classics from his father. Afterward he studied in a newly formed Palace School, where the hours were long, the protocol strict, and the education orthodox. Like other Chinese schoolboys, he first learned the traditional texts by heart, without any explanation. It was his duty, he was told, not to forget them. He later said, "Prior to ascending the throne, I had thoroughly got by heart the Six Classics and the various histories. Since assuming the responsibilities of State I have had far less free time but have not stopped examining the Classics and studying the rites." But the old literature of China attracted him far less than its history, in which he found the lessons an Emperor really had to know. He was particularly, even obsessively, attracted to the figure of the seventh-century Emperor of T'ang China, T'ai-tsung, after whom he hoped to model himself.

Ch'ien-lung's student essays, which were published and then elaborated and republished as an inspiration to others, show him in the light of a proper Confucian ruler. A proper Confucian ruler is invariably moderate, diligent, prepared to take advice, and respectful toward heaven and man alike. He is a sage rather than a despot. Harsh, impetuous rule, says Ch'ien-lung, leads to ruin, whereas magnanimity wins gratitude and submission. The most crucial task of the Emperor, he thinks, is to find the right men to help him rule. He, the ruler, is their superior; but he and they can be one at heart and, through this very oneness, can create social harmony everywhere.*

The Examination Life

The political and intellectual culture of China became rooted, as time went on, in a unique Chinese institution, the examination system. This system, on which all the

* It would be amusing and perhaps enlightening to compare Ch'ien-lung's education with that of his near-contemporary, Louis XIV, the model of European kings. Louis' teachers succeeded in making him an accomplished French gentleman, but not a scholar. He never became much interested in Classical, *i.e.*, Greek and Roman literature, nor, in fact, in any literature. But he was thoroughly conscientious and as protocol-conscious as a Chinese emperor. Like Ch'ien-lung, he tried to learn from history and insisted that he could not make decisions unless he were thoroughly well-informed. Again like Ch-ien-lung, he emphasized the importance of ruling, as far as possible, by gentleness and persuasion, and, like him, considered that the choice of men to help him was crucial. Like any Confucian or simply decent king, Louis insisted that "all people are bound together by reciprocal responsibilities," the obedience and respect of the subjects being given in exchange for the justice and protection of the king. See J. B. Wolf, *Louis XIV*, London, Gollancz, 1968.

levels of formal education were based, was designed, as has been said already, to furnish a loyal, effective bureaucracy. By all historic precedents, the empire of China should have crumbled into its constituent fragments. It was too enormous, varied, and complex to last; and yet it did last, changing shape, retracting, breaking, and forming again, longer than any comparable empire. There is no clear reason for this persistence other than the bureaucracy, with its examination system and Confucian ideology. The almost utopian impression that the scholar-bureaucracy could make on Europeans is evident in the words of Matthew Ricci, the sixteenth-century Jesuit. He was especially struck by the un-European relationship between scholars and soldiers:

> The entire kingdom is administered by the Order of the Learned, commonly known as The Philosophers. The responsibility for orderly management of the entire realm is wholly and completely committed to their care. The army, both officers and soldiers, hold them in high respect and show them the promptest obedience and deference, and not infrequently the military are disciplined by them as a schoolboy might be punished by his master. . . . The Philosophers far excel military leaders in the good will and respect of the people and in opportunities of acquiring wealth. What is still more surprising to strangers is that these same Philosophers, as they are called, with respect to nobility of sentiment and in contempt of danger and death, where fidelity to King and country is concerned, surpass even those whose particular profession is the defense of the fatherland.

The beginnings of the examination system go back at least two centuries B.C. About 140 B.C., we hear of a provincial governor, Wen Wang, who selected able minor officials and, after having them trained at the capital, made them teachers of other candidates for office. In 124 B.C., Emperor Han Wu Ti established an Imperial Academy with fifty government-supported students, who were given official posts if they were successful in their studies. This academy, like the whole examination system, had a checkered history; but in the course of time graded schools of higher learning were established, libraries assembled, and student dormitories built. By the middle of the second cen-

16

tury A.D., the schools had thirty thousand students. Schools and examination system developed together until, in the 1890s, some two million candidates would take the examination every year. Only a small fraction, perhaps one or two percent, would pass.

The system, as it existed in the nineteenth century, was based on three major sets of examinations and three titles or "degrees," each degree corresponding to one of the examination sets. Anyone passing the first, district examination would be considered a Government Student, or, more colloquially, a Budding Talent. A Government Student was addressed with especial courtesy, exempted from the labor tax, and given an honorable status in his village. But he was not yet eligible for office and may be considered a commoner.

The second, provincial examination led to the degree of Recommended Man, *chü-jen*, a "man sent up" to the next examination. A Recommended Man could get minor official positions. No longer a commoner, he wore a distinctive gown and a hat with a gold button.

The third, metropolitan examination led to the degree of Metropolitan Graduate, *chin-shih*, a "scholar admitted" to the palace for final examination. He was considered an official of the middle rank and was appointed as a magistrate, assistant secretary of a government board, or the like. If especially successful in the palace examination, he was sent on to the Han-lin Academy, the august institution where future high officials were trained and ceremonial texts for imperial use prepared.

As can be imagined, the examination life was prolonged and difficult. The average age of Government Students was about twenty-four, of Recommended Men about thirty, and of Metropolitan Graduates about thirty-five. But many candidates sat for these examinations for twenty or thirty years or more. At the age of eighty or ninety, candidates who had failed repeatedly might be given a consolation degree. They were failures, but honorable ones.

The examinations were of course given on a large scale. Thousands of students would gather at a special building, where they were searched for notes and locked from dawn to dusk in little cells, each with a table and seat. It is not surprising that some examinees and even examiners chose the occasion to go mad. Many precautions were taken to ensure fairness. For example, while the answers were being read, the examiners were not allowed to talk to one another. Often the answers were recopied by scribes so that the examiners should not recognize the name or handwriting of any candidate.

In spite of all precautions, there was cheating, and sometimes, it seems, a great deal of it. When examinations decided the whole of a man's career, bribery was to be expected. Sometimes the scribes were bribed to pass the candidates' names on to the examiners, who were bribed in turn. Or candidates might pass on clues so that the examiners could identify their papers. Expert stand-ins were hired; questions and answers were thrown back and forth over the cell walls; and clothing was lined with thousands of microscopically written essays to which the "padded" candidate had an index.

Sometimes, at least in the nineteenth century, there was a complete breakdown of morality. In a report of 1877, we can read that in spite of open cheating "the prince and high officials who were supposed to supervise the examination watched and snickered, not appearing to have been surprised or shocked at all." A certain proportion of the lower degrees were in any case sold by the government. This practice was already in existence in the sixteenth century, but in the second half of the eighteenth, when the government was particularly short of money, it became widespread.

The examinations themselves were on the Confucian Classics, social morality, poetry, and, toward the end, philology. The candidate had to write both poems and essays. The most important part of the examination was usually an essay on a moral theme taken from one of the Confucian Classics. The length of the essay was set at a maximum, perhaps, of seven hundred words. An "Analysis of the Theme" was supposed to be followed by an "Amplification of the Theme," and this followed by a more extended "Explanation" and a "Post-Explanation." An examination essay of this sort is disappointing when translated. The clever hints and disciplined style dissolve into triviality.

18

The Chinese were not invariably happy with their examination system. It was often defended, as by the eleventh-century poet, Su Tung-po, by the argument that it had produced good officials and statesmen. But Wang An-shih, Su's contemporary and enemy, argued that concentration on poetry and on the composition of rhyming couplets denies an official just the knowledge that he will need in practice. Another famous attack was made by Ku Yen-wu, in the seventeenth century. He argued that the stereotyped writing encouraged by the examination could not be good. Furthermore, he said, the examinations encourage, not critical thinking, but mere memorizing and orthodoxy. The students were basically out for themselves, he said, and added, "It is these students who know the secrets of officialdom and trade with them. . . . With the slightest rebuff, they cry out, 'You are killing the scholars. You are burying Confucianists!' "

For years now, scholars have been carrying on an animated debate on the merits of the examination system. Although the debate is far from closed, the evidence seems to call for a rather favorable verdict. Some of its faults have been enumerated. Even apart from the possibilities of bribing, of buying degrees, or of belonging to a favored category, there was a certain favoritism built into the system. The sons of educated men acquired an education more easily than others, and the sons of the rich could hire the more capable teachers. A scholar's house was saturated with learning, a peasant's empty of it.*

* In order not to compare the Chinese system with a merely abstract ideal, I should like to cite two contemporary criticisms, the first of education in the United States, and the second of education in France.

According to the first criticism:

"It seems plausible—indeed inevitable—that parents with professional jobs and higher degrees make their children feel that staying in college is worth almost any sacrifice, since dropping out permanently will probably mean downward mobility. Conversely, those whose parents are poorly educated make their children feel that dropping out, while unfortunate, is not a disaster. . . . Most children born in poor homes grow up with limited vocabularies, limited contact with adults, and limited contact with intellectually stimulating teachers or classmates. They have no privacy, no quiet, no possibility of concentrating on any problem without interruption, be it homework or building blocks. As time goes on they fall increasingly behind their upper-middle class fellows, suffering intellectual damage which

19

The evidence tells us, not surprisingly, that the sons of scholar-officials were favored; but once a commoner was appointed to an official post, he rose, it seems, just as quickly as the son of a member of the elite. The evidence tells us that, in the nineteenth century, almost two-thirds of the Metropolitan Graduates came from the families of simple commoners or of Government Students, the more respected of the commoners. There are, furthermore, many examples of rural men who rose from degree to degree.

A concrete example will show how the ambitious son of a sixteenth-century farmer was able to rise by means of the examination system. The man in question is one Ch'i Hsien, who became a Metropolitan Graduate in 1526. We are told that his great-grandfather, when dying at the age of ninety-two, sobbed out, "It is not Heaven's will that my family should have failed to produce a single degree holder, let alone high officials!" But his envy of the high officials he had seen in the capital bore fruit only three generations later, in Ch'i Hsien.

Ch'i Hsien, [we read,] being young and feeble, could not stand heavy field work, but was intelligent and fond of studies. As a little boy he heard from his elders what his great-grandfather had said on his deathbed. He was saddened and humiliated, and vowed to become established. His father, however, disliked study and often ordered him to carry a heavy load. He entreated that he be exempted from strenuous physical labor but to no avail. His mother often sobbed together with him. A

is both cumulative and progressively harder to remedy" (C. Jencks & D. Reisman, *The Academic Revolution*, Garden City, Doubleday & Co., 1968, pp. 120, 125).

According to the second criticism, on France:

"Strange as it may seem, education in France is in many ways even more closely divided on class lines than in Britain with its public schools. The State *lycées*, though in theory free and open to all, are in practice still largely a preserve of the middle class, and they alone provide a passport to higher education and the best jobs. The percentage of workers' children who go to university is slowly rising but is still little more than 1 per cent, much less than in Britain. . . . According to one recent survey, of the 2,530 most famous or powerful people in France today, from de Gaulle to Sylvie Varton, only 3 per cent have come from working-class homes, while 68 per cent of France's ruling élite is recruited from the top 5 per cent of the population" (J. Ardagh, *The New French Revolution*, London, Secker & Warburg, 1968, p. 233).

neighboring elder found this out and offered Ch'i Hsien room and board so that he could study.

Shortly after the turn of the fifteenth century Ch'üan-chiao county was short of people who could be enlisted for clerical work at the magistrate's office. Some local-government underlings tried to draft Ch'i Hsien. He entreated his father once more to be allowed to take the *sheng-yüan* (Government Student) examination in order to avoid lowly clerical work. His father at last gave in and stopped interfering with his studies. In two years Ch'i Hsien obtained his *sheng-yüan* degree.

Because of the number of people to be fed, the family was now poor. Ch'i Hsien contracted tuberculosis, a result of prolonged malnutrition. His mother's death dealt him a further blow. He lay in bed for several years before he finally recovered and married at the age of 29. He was one of the two *sheng-yüan* of the locality chosen to supervise famine relief in 1522. The next year for the first time he came across the writings of the great philosopher-statesman Wang Yang-ming, which opened up a new intellectual vista for him. Thereafter he acquired an unusual fluency of thought which greatly helped his literary composition. In 1525 he passed the provincial examination held in Nanking and in the following year he became a *chin-shih*. He eventually reached the office of supervisor of the Board of Punishments (rank 5a).

When it is asked whether or not the examination system was successful, it is hard to give a simple answer. The immediate temptation is to answer with a question, "The examination system in what respects? and where? and when?" It had its best times and worst, its cultured, conscientious products, and its ultra-conformist and corrupt ones. It was certainly a major factor in the great prestige of traditional literature, and the correspondingly low prestige of many other occupations, including intellectual ones. Matthew Ricci, speaking of the sixteenth-century China he knew, says, "The study of mathematics and that of medicine are held in low esteem, because they are not fostered by honors as is the study of philosophy, to which students are attracted by the hope of the glory and rewards attached to it. This may be readily seen in the interest taken in the study of moral philosophy. The man who is promoted to the higher degrees in this field, prides himself on the fact that he has in truth attained to the pinnacle of Chinese happiness."

Late in the nineteenth century, the examination system more or less collapsed. There were many reasons. One was the great increase in population, which increased, in turn, the number of students, the competition for appointments, and the corruption of those who made the appointments.

But if we compare the examination system across the centuries with the system or lack of system in other countries, if we regard the richness of Chinese culture as in some ways dependent upon the maintenance of an orderly empire, then such ambitions as the system satisfied, such honor as it earned for literature, such conscientiousness as it fathered at its best, and such social mobility as it did afford, make of it an almost unbelievably successful human institution.*

Tension,
Sensitivity,
and Art

The examination system had an enormous influence on cultured men. Every one of them located himself in life by his position on the examination ladder, or, occasionally, by his conscious refusal to climb it. He might try and fail, might tire, might disdain to try, or might, having endangered himself or grown old, retire from climbing. But he could not really forget the ladder. A seventeenth-century scholar, explaining why a certain Wang family was successful, made it easy to see how a constant psychological pressure was being exerted on its members:

Those who have attained official ranks are resplendent in official hats and sashes, those who have failed in examinations are doomed to wear short [commoners'] jackets. This sharp

---

* In the West, too, civil servants have often been chosen on the basis of their general, not specialized education. Perhaps the best-known example is the Classical education of British officials, which has been justified on humanistic grounds. Western government officials are still involved in the dilemma of "generalists" versus "specialists."

contrast in status makes the laggards ashamed. Therefore the father instructs the son, the wife urges her husband that everybody must study hard and make good in examinations and officialdom. That is why the Wang clan has produced so many holders of higher degrees and officials and has become a clan of national renown.

Men literate enough to climb the examination ladder might easily develop an interest in literature outside the examination curriculum. But writing, like art, was not looked upon as an exclusive career for an educated man. His career was exclusively in public service, and his writing, calligraphy, or painting could be no more than an appropriate avocation. Connoisseurship, it is true, became increasingly ceremonial. Viewing a collector's pictures took on the air of a rite. In an atmosphere pervaded by incense, the guests washed their hands in large brass bowls, and only then turned to the pictures. Although wine was usual in literary gatherings, etiquette demanded that fragrant tea, and not wine, should be the drink that enhanced the enjoyment of picture-scrolls. (See Plate IV.)

But even such connoisseurship was often only the enhancement of a public life. When an interest in literature or art became exclusive, when it led to neglect of the practical goal of life, which was the strengthening of the family's position and the increase of its wealth, it was regarded as a destructive self-indulgence. Such self-indulgence became increasingly frequent in the Ch'ien-lung era. The number of collectors grew, and their passion grew with their number. As a result, one of the stock figures of the age was the collector, the son of a wealthy family of scholar-officials, who dissipated the family fortune. A contemporary observer said, "If a rich or landowning family has a son who loves literature, art, and music, he will almost surely impoverish the family."

Practical success or failure apart, educated men were esthetes. Their autobiographies reveal what we should in any case guess. Examinations and official career could never, of course, be forgotten. But to the surprise of the Westerner, matters he would consider essential—relations, for example, with parents—were slighted, while the occasions on which poetry was composed or beauty experienced were remembered. This was, so to speak, the proper content and style of memory. (See Plates V and VI.)

Recalling his childhood, Shen Fu, an eighteenth-century writer and painter, said, "I remember that when I was a small boy I would stare into the sun with wide-open eyes. I remember, too, that I could see very clearly such minute autumn hairs as the down on plants and the markings on the tiniest insects. I loved to look closely at anything delicate or small; examining the grains of pieces of wood, the veins and patterns of leaves or the streaks and lines on some insignificant trifle, gave me an almost magical delight."

Literature was rich and available enough for a sensitive, dreamy child to fall in love with books. In a seventeenth-century collection of stories, there is one about "The Crazy Book Worm." He read, we are told, not to gain office, but, in keeping with a traditional verse, to find "gold and grain" in his books. Day and night, winter and summer, year in and year out, he read. Instead of marrying, he waited for some beauty to step out of a book. How this finally happened cannot be told here. The point is only that this story reflects the possibility of living outside of the cold, competitive world and inside the easy, romantic fantasies of books.

Yuan Mei, the great eighteenth-century poet, never rid himself of his youthful love for books. He was saddened by the failure of his children to share it. In a poem of memory and regret he wrote:

I remember how when I was only eleven or twelve
I loved books more than life itself.
Whenever I came to a stall where books were sold
I read and read, my feet rooted where I stood.
But always I had no money to buy books;
I could only dream I had bought them, when I came home.
Yet of all the notes and extracts I still possess,
More than half were made in those early days.
When I got a post and had money to spend
I bought so many that they filled the whole house.
Now that I am old I still read them at night,
Not stopping till I have burnt a whole candle.
My boys, at the age I was then,
Look at a book without the least emotion. . . .

24

The sensitivity of so many Chinese scholars to nature and their love for books may seem to need no special explanation. Perhaps they do not; but apart from the very presence of art and books and parents who loved them both, there was, I suspect, a familiar but half-concealed reason. The child's life of polite submission was too hard to bear, and so the filial son and son-like official had to retreat. Retreat to what? To Taoism, Buddhism, painting, calligraphy, and literature, to the outlaw heroes of plays and novels, and to wine and even gambling.

The latent antagonism of the sons broke into the open in the early twentieth century, when the Confucian tradition came under an attack that was to prove fatal. The reformer, Hu Shih, wrote bitterly, "All the much-idealized virtues of filial piety simply could not exist; and in those cases where they were consciously cultivated, the price paid for them was nothing short of intense suppression, resulting in mental and physical agony." With at least equal bitterness, the writer, Lu Hsün, recalled in a story that his elder brother had taught him that a child was obligated to feed an ill parent on its own boiled flesh, and that he himself must have participated in cannibalistic family meals. The memory prompted him to hope that there were still some infants that had not yet eaten men, and to cry out, "Save, save the infants!"

I cannot forbear breaking the tension of Lu Hsün's cry by repeating a joke current at the time among the more conservative Chinese, the anti-anti-Confucians. They said that the old proverb, "Adultery is the first of all sins, and filial piety the first of all virtues" was being transformed into, "Filial piety is the first of all sins, and adultery the first of all virtues."

Hu Shih and Lu Hsün were men of rebellious temperament in a revolutionary situation. Others found the rewards of Confucian piety greater and its pains less. A Confucian family good in its own terms was able to give both physical and psychological security. A member of such a great family-organism would not be abandoned to himself. He knew who he was and what he had to do, and he had little of the solitary European's need to find himself in Promethean acts.

It was comforting, then, to belong to a Confucian family, but very tiring. You were always having to check your natural aggressiveness. In the worse cases, it was like always being on the verge of a headache, your courtesy masking your anger. The Chinese needed a way to rest from the strain and to restore the contact between their outer, courteous faces and their inner, immediate selves. The emotions that had been hidden beyond acknowledgment could not be directly expressed. But the Chinese were able to express them in the stylized forms of their art. The brush that shaped words and landscape contours was the instrument by which their vitality was allowed and their wholeness preserved.

2
Artists

INSPIRATION AND

CONVENTION

ALL of us share the Chinese problem of reconciling a primitive inner self with a conventional outer one. In the simply human nature that we share, we are as Chinese as the Chinese themselves. But it is easy to exaggerate or minimize the likeness between our nature and theirs. To know them better, we have to look closer at the evidence. Much of it has been left by the artists of China, and so we shall call them now as witnesses. First, however, a general word on their art.

To a Westerner, Chinese painting may seem too pale and too uniform. It especially lacks the geometrical perspective, the anatomical knowledge, and the thickness and brightness of oil paint, all of which came to Europe with the Renaissance. Yet if, like Chinese connoisseurs of the last dynasties, we look back at the whole of Chinese painting, it becomes, within its limitations, astonishingly rich. The range of its subject matter is wider than that of Renaissance Europe. For the Chinese have their religious pictures, historical scenes, portraits, and genre pictures, their animals, birds, insects, flowers, fruits, trees, and landscapes. They have few nudes, it is true, and their leading artists have often considered portraiture to be beneath them. Their skill and sensitivity have been exercised instead on the face and body of the earth.

I have listed these subjects as they entered my mind. A more discriminating and Chinese classification might be as follows:

First, landscape, which is to say, mountains and water; and also, usually, trees.

29

Second, men and objects. This includes the subclasses of ceremonial, mostly posthumous portraits; life portraits; beautiful women; Taoist and Buddhist saints; genre paintings of local customs, festivals, and so on; illustrations of historical events; illustrations of stories or legends; erotic pictures; and curios or antiques.

Third, birds and animals. Fishes and dragons are a more or less separate class, not on a par with the other animal subjects.

Fourth, flowers and plants. Included in this class are annuals and perennials that grow new stalks every year; plants, such as peonies, with permanent woody stems or trunks; "broken branches"—flowers, sprays, or branches separated from the parent stalk; and grasses and insects.

The range of style and technique in Chinese painting is no less great than that of subject matter. There is dynamism and there is stillness. There are styles of nervous conciseness and of careful fullness. Some paintings are purposely crude or bare, and others just as purposely elegant or rich. The concentration in some paintings on isolated things, a bamboo or a blade of grass, does not prevent others from having a fully worked out environment, with plane behind plane, until, in the last dynasty, a landscape can be composed of interlocking, polyphonic spaces.

A Chinese painting may be made up of dots like those of a pointillist, of irregular splashes of ink, or of a graded mist; or it may be dominated by strong, purposeful lines. Sometimes it is pushed into a corner of the silk, sometimes centered, or, more often, balanced, shape against shape, around an off-center axis. Although a freely drawn line is more usual, a mechanical, ruled line is used for architecture. Drawings are made in unvarying wiry outlines, and in the sensitive thickening and thinning of Chinese calligraphy. Monochrome is favored, but many paintings have strong blue-greens or patches of bright color.

If we consider techniques from a more Chinese point of view, an abbreviated classification might be:

Spontaneous sketch; detailed, precise, usually colored painting; academic painting; blue and green landscape; the same, but with the color dominating the outlines and texture strokes; gold-outlined landscape; lightly, usually umber-colored ink painting; somewhat more deeply, usually purplish red-colored ink painting; uncolored ink painting; "broken ink" painting, defined in outline and built up with texture strokes; "spilled ink" painting, in broad strokes and without outlines; dry brush painting; and "flying white," with the hairs of the brush separated to make streaks.

As we can sense from the Chinese classification, the Chinese practice a conscious, detailed realism, though this must be understood in relation to their conventions. They also practice a realism that tries to capture essences rather than appearances. Finally, they sometimes care far more for the displayed consciousness of the painter than for the subject he may be supposed to have painted. As for degrees of originality, there are the genuinely individual painters, the eclectic assemblers of different styles, the makers of variations on accepted styles and themes, the careful imitators, and the outright forgers. (See Plates VII and VIII.)

The painters themselves are a varied lot. They include artisans, monks, professionals, Academicians, gentlemen-scholars, and those who, for want of a better name, we shall set down as eccentrics. In temperament, there are the matter-of-fact, the gregarious, the sensitive, the sad wanderers in the mist, the deliberately obscene, and the near-madmen.

The painters display the whole range of Chinese views of life. Most writers on Chinese painting stress Taoism and Ch'an Buddhism. But all Chinese views, including, certainly, the varieties of Confucianism, mingle and form the Chinese cosmos, within which the emphases are less those that a philosophical or religious dogma makes for the person than those that he makes for himself. A traditional Chinese may *believe* almost everything or almost nothing, though everything is more likely than nothing, in whatever combination he pleases. But he may, of course, not *do* what he pleases, even within the limits of the law, unless he is a certified eccentric. One of the great attractions of art in China must therefore have been the tolerance of eccentricity in artists.

Ku K'ai-chih,
the First
Knowable Painter

How far back can we go in studying the Chinese artists? If we are concerned with recognizable individuals, the answer is to the fourth century A.D., to Ku K'ai-chih (344?–406?). He is the first Chinese painter whose life, opinions, and works we can read about in the sources, and whose style we can see, at least reflected in copies, with our own eyes.

The best-known work attributed to Ku K'ai-chih is the *Admonitions of the Instructress to the Palace Ladies*, now in the British Museum. A scroll, it consists of a series of illustrations to a moral text. One picture, for example, is in praise of the concubine, Lady Feng, who saved the Emperor by thrusting herself between him and a wild bear. Another shows Lady Pan, who spared the Emperor distraction and scandal by refusing his invitation to ride with him in his litter. A third demonstrates that the Emperor abandons one concubine in favor of another, which drives home the lesson that no one can always remain in favor. These scenes are drawn in an even, supple, unhesitating line. The expressions of the people are slight but convincing. Although the stories it illustrates may sound humorous to us, the scroll has a severe style.

Ku K'ai-chih's biography, preserved in the *History of the Chin Dynasty*, contradicts one of the morals he illustrated, for he survived the deadly Court politics and remained in constant favor. Educated Chinese have come to cherish each of his supposed remarks and eccentricities as part of their cultural history. Though I have had to abbreviate it, his biography is therefore repeated here:

K'ai-chih had wide knowledge and the spark of genius.

When K'ai-chih ate sugar cane, he usually chewed it from the end to the middle. When the people wondered why, he would say, "One enters into the realm of delights gradually."

K'ai-chih excelled in the art of "red and green" (color painting), and was distinguished especially for his portraits. Premier Hsieh An valued his art and averred, "There has been nothing like it since the birth of man."

When he completed the painting of a human figure, he often waited several years before he would touch up the pupils. When asked for an explanation, he would answer, "The beauty or ugliness of the limbs and body is in fact all there without fault. But the subtle point where the spirit can be rendered and perfect likeness portrayed lies just in those little spots."

Once he admired a girl in his neighborhood and enticed her, but she would not yield. He then painted her likeness on a wall, and pierced a thorn-needle into its heart. Thereupon the girl suffered from heartache. K'ai-chih took the opportunity to express his tender solicitude. The girl yielded to his wish. Then he secretly removed the needle and the girl was well.

He greatly valued Hsi K'ang's four-character line poems, and took them as themes for his paintings. Often he commented,

"It is easy to paint his
'Hand plucking the five strings,'
but not his
'Eyes meanwhile following the homeward-faring geese.' "

The portraits that K'ai-chih painted had a subtlety unequalled in his time. Once he painted a portrait of P'ei K'ai and added three hairs to the jaw, so that the spectators felt an extraordinary effect of some divine intelligence about the features.

K'ai-chih once entrusted Huan Hsüan with paintings contained in a chest, the front of which he pasted up with a label. These were all his dearly treasured pieces. Hsüan, however, pried open the back of the chest, took all the paintings, and, after careful repair, returned the chest to him and hoaxed him, saying, "I never opened it." When he discovered that the chest was sealed by the same label as before but all the paintings were gone, K'ai-chih promptly said, "The marvellous works partook of divine power, transformed themselves and vanished, like men ascending to join the immortals." He showed not the slightest surprise.

K'ai-chih was full of vainglory, and young beaus therefore amused themselves and mocked him by echoing his self-praise. His headquarters were next to that of Hsieh Chan. One night he chanted poems under the moon. Chan occasionally applauded him from a distance. So K'ai-chih kept on with greater effort, unaware of fatigue. Chan himself went to sleep, but put a substitute there to continue the applause. K'ai-chih could not sense any difference and went on chanting till dawn.

Formerly, when he was on Huan Wen's staff, the latter used to say that in K'ai-chih intelligence and folly each formed one half of the man, and that the two parts judged together would strike a nice balance. Therefore, popular tradition has it that K'ai-chih was unexcelled in three ways: as a wit, as a painter, and as a fool.

He died in office, at the age of sixty-two [by Chinese count].

Ku K'ai-chih's biography shows a number of traits common to Chinese artists.

It shows pride. Chinese courtesy is elaborate, and both Confucianism and Taoism are against egoistic display; but in China, as elsewhere, pride could easily be displayed in manners that were superficially modest. I think, for a reason I shall later explain, that much of the scholar-art of China has undertones of depression. But depression and pride can join, even fiercely, as we see in modern artists. Chinese artists valued themselves as unique, creative individuals. When, as we read, they abandoned pictures, it was because the creative act and personality were important to them, not the pictures. Too proud to sell his art, the scholar-painter might become too proud to give it away to the people who besieged him. They were no more to him than buyers once removed, not attuned to his pure soul, and more interested in objects than in the vitality concentrated in the artist's gesture.

The biography shows the atmosphere of sport and competitiveness in which Chinese artists might live. Even originality, that is to say, the ability to improvise, was subject to public demonstration and connoisseurs loved to recall the prodigies of improvisation that had won historic contests—to avoid long explanations, I have omitted the story of the verse-contest in which Ku K'ai-chih took part. There was, of course, an immediate prize for success in contests, but the essential prize, I think, was fame. Artists were aware of history and must often have had the ambition to be immortalized in it. Nor did they forget that distinction as a painter or poet could earn a post in the government.

The biography shows that even in the fourth century the artist might be a valued member of the court, occupying official positions there, and nevertheless—if this is the right word—famous for his eccentricities.

It shows that the poet and the painter might be the

34

same person; that paintings were made to accompany poems; and that clever suggestiveness was valued.

It shows the belief that there were seemingly slight but crucial acts, such as the placing of the lights in the eyes or forceful sketching of a few hairs, that infused vitality into a painting. Paintings could be the magical equivalents of living things, or even themselves alive. Ku K'ai-chih's painting of a Buddhist saint is said to have filled the whole monastery hall with radiance.

Finally, the *Admonitions of the Instructress* shows that painting can have a moral aim.

The Life-Breath

About a century after the death of Ku K'ai-chih, Hsieh Ho tried to put the essential characteristics of painting into six brief formulas, each consisting of two two-word phrases. It is sometimes assumed that the second phrase of each formula explains the first. If we make this assumption, and if we translate with the perhaps misleading literalness we use to decipher important old texts, we may get:

FIRST: Reverberation of the life-breath; that is, the creation of movement.
SECOND: Bone-method; that is, the proper use of the brush.
THIRD: Reflection of the objects; that is, the depiction of forms.
FOURTH: Respect for types; that is, the application of colors.
FIFTH: Layout of the design; that is, the arrangement of positions.
SIXTH: Transmission and perpetuation; that is, the copying of old models.

If we translate more naturally, more in keeping with the immediate response of an educated Chinese, we may get:

FIRST: Creating a lifelike tone and atmosphere.
SECOND: Building structure through brush-work.
THIRD: Depicting the forms of things as they are.
FOURTH: Appropriate coloring.
FIFTH: Composition.
SIXTH: Transcribing and copying.

Of these essential characteristics, much the most important in later discussions was the first. Its Chinese words are, *ch'i yün, shêng tung. Ch'i* is the breath of life that is believed to animate nature. It can be translated "force," or "natural force." *Yün* is "resonance," "reverberation," or "harmonious consonance." The translation, "tone," fits its application to painting. Literally, then, *ch'i yün* may be taken to mean "the reverberation of the universal breath of life." The words, or the bisyllabic word, *shêng tung*, would then explain that the reverberation of the universal breath of life was equivalent to "the creation of movement." Another possibility is the translation, "The reverberation of breath of life creates life-movement."*

Enough of attempts to translate. The principle can be explained by the use made of it and by the successive reactions to it of the Chinese painters. At first, as we have seen in the stories about Ku K'ai-chih, the principle seems to have meant that the force of nature could be transferred into a painting, which would come somehow alive. Wu Tao-tzu, a quick-tempered, tipsy genius of the eighth century, is said to have painted dragons so alive that they seemed to be moving their scales. More impressively, they would give off mist before it rained outside. His equal mastery of the six essentials was such that he could paint a figure "with the blood circulating under the skin." His scenes of Hell are said to have frightened visitors into decency and charity.

The inner force and moral aim of art were often thought to be compatible with realism. It is not un-Chinese to want to be accurate to the facts. One sixth-century painter, Yao Tsui, even complained that fashions in clothing changed so quickly that a painter found it hard to keep his paintings from becoming outdated. Later, in the tenth

* Such translator's quibbles can eventually be interesting and illuminating. The most careful analysis I know of Hsieh Ho's essentials is in W. R. B. Acker, *Some T'ang and Pre-T'ang Texts on Chinese Painting*, Leiden, E. J. Brill, 1954, pp. xiv-xliii. The literal translation I have used is from O. Siren, *Chinese Painting, Leading Masters and Principles*, London, Lund Humphries, 1956, I, 5. Lin Yutang, whose translation I have quoted above as the "response of an educated Chinese," makes some acid comments on the unfamiliarity of many Sinologists with Chinese. See his book, *The Chinese Theory of Art*, London, Heinemann, 1967, pp. 34-38.

century, Ou-yang Chiung warned that neither life nor formal likeness could be neglected. Eleventh-century flower painters are said to have taken pride in their ability to paint flowers so exact in every detail that even laymen could recognize their species. The eleventh-century painter, Mi Fei or Mi Fu (1051–1107), suggested an odd compromise with realism. Landscapes, he said, must come from the heart, but everything else need only be accurate. He complained that painters made themselves ridiculous by the inaccuracy with which they portrayed ancient costumes.

The Emperor Hui-tsung (1101–1125), himself a painter, was a stickler for accuracy. He wanted his artists to notice which leg a pheasant lifts first when it climbs up a rock—it was the left, he said. He required them to distinguish the seasonal appearances of petals and leaves and, like a very Monet, their hourly appearances. He gave a reward for a rose painted exactly as it appears on the noon-hour of a spring day.

The argument of those who believed that accuracy and life go together was put neatly by Nan-t'ien (Yün Shou-p'ing) in the seventeenth century. A flower painter himself, he criticized others of his kind for their arbitrary license. "They seem to think," he said, "that art consists in altering nature. I on the other hand believe that it is only by pushing truthful representation to its absolute limits that one can transmit the inner essence of a flower's being."

In spite of the desire of some painters to be realistic, others preferred to distinguish between outer resemblance and essential, inner likeness. The distinction is clear in the words of Chang Yen-yüan, of the mid-ninth century. Modern pictures, he says, are more brilliant and detailed than the ancient ones, but they are as meaningless as if made by a mere artisan. Modern painters can capture outward appearances fairly well, but where is the life-breath, where is Ku K'ai-chih's wind-gust of a brush stroke, which transmitted ideas that had existed *before* he had picked up his brush? Every stroke of the brush should reveal life. Wu Tao-tzu's pictures seem unfinished, yet they express his ideas fully. Painters should be afraid, not of apparent incompleteness, but of a too literal completeness.

The Great Message
of Forests and
Streams

The fullest, most revealing essay by a Chinese painter is *The Great Message of Forests and Streams*. The essay was compiled by the son of the eleventh-century painter, Kuo Hsi, to record his father's practices and opinions. Technical advice apart, what does it say?

Cultivated men love landscapes. They feel light and free in them. But in times of peace they cannot go off and live alone. They are responsible to the ruler and to their parents, and they have to leave the forest to dreams. A good painter, however, can reproduce a landscape for us and set us among its streams and ravines, the cries of monkeys and calls of birds in our ears. There in our homes, we are struck by the light on the mountains and the water's reflected colors, and our dreams are fulfilled.

Some landscapes, real or painted, are good for traveling through or far-off contemplation; but the best are those good for walking and living in.

Learning to paint is like learning calligraphy. One should study different models and schools and combine them to form a personal style. To specialize too narrowly as a painter is to be like the musician who harps on one note all the time. People have always taken pleasure in the new, and a master will therefore not limit himself to a single style or school.

Like everything else, painting has its secret rules. Whatever he represents, the painter should concentrate on its essential nature and so focus his spirit. Spirit and work must be fused. If the painter does not fuse them, if he is lazy and only forces himself to work, his strokes will be soft and indecisive. If he is sluggish and works in a disorderly way, his forms become obscure and lacking in vigor. If he works too light-heartedly, his forms will be unsteady and sketchy. If conceit makes him careless, his style will be lax and coarse.

The subject of a painting, to be experienced, must be observed attentively. If it is to be experienced completely, a flower, for example, should be put into a hole in the ground and studied from above. And the real shape of a bamboo should be observed in the shadow its moonlit stalk casts on a white wall.

The effects of landscapes, of the seasonally changing clouds and mists, the wind and rain, and the light and shadow, can be grasped most clearly when seen from afar. From close by, they are fragmentary.

Mountains should be arranged around the majestic mountain, their lord, like courtiers around an emperor; but the emperor should not be arrogant. The leader among trees is the tall pine. It is a superior, contented and successful among its subordinates, which it causes no annoyance.

To look at a painting is to feel that one is really in the mountains. When one has studied the famous mountains, wandered among them, satiated one's eyes with them, and stored them in one's mind, then, with eyes unconscious of the silk before them and hand unconscious of brush and ink, the picture is created, marvelous, mysterious, boundless.

The mountains have arteries, their watercourses; and hair, the grass and trees; and an atmosphere of beauty, the mist and clouds. Flowing water, grass and trees, mist and clouds, these are the mountains' life, beauty, and allure. "Mountains without mist and clouds are like a spring without flowers and grass."

The water, too, is a living thing. It has mountains for a face, pavillions for eyes and eyebrows, and the activity of fishing for animation.

Rocks, the bones of heaven and earth, are precious, and should be buried deeply. Water, the blood of heaven and earth, is precious, and should circulate freely, without obstruction.

The inner mood needed to give shape to ideas comes only when one is perfectly harmonious. Only when the circumstances are ripe and the heart and mind responsive are the horizontal and vertical strokes true. "Then the people of the world will be moved and enabled roughly to grasp my intentions."

This essay is, I think, true to the usual Chinese attitudes. It contains all the feelings, without any extremism, that normally would be found together. The technical advice is given, the nostalgia for a lonely peace is recalled, the moral analogy is pressed, in Chinese style, and the world is assumed to be a living thing, almost a great, indeterminate man. The artist is expected to be at once in communion with nature, with himself, and with his silk and brush, in that state of unstrained alertness in which he can recreate the landscape. From the sincerity of his heart to the spontaneity of his brush, to the live depth of the landscape, the world is joined.

Spontaneity

I have been emphasizing sincerity and spontaneity. Sincerity, the accord of heart and action, is a noticeably Confucian virtue. Spontaneity, however, is more a Taoist virtue, and inasmuch as a Taoist may take it to mean that he should disregard convention, it is not the same as Confucian sincerity or harmony, and it can be expressed in more radical words than those of Kuo Hsi. In China, spontaneity takes surprising forms, refined and unrefined. This is shown especially well by the Neo-Taoists of the third and fourth centuries, who believed in living in ways that were natural or spontaneous, and not subservient to moral rules. Some of them made it their nonmoral rule to follow every impulse. Liu Ling, at home in the universe, stayed naked in his room. The universe, he said, was his home, the room his clothing, and with these words he invited visiting critics to get out of his pants. The Juan family, just as Neo-Taoistic, were drinkers, and when they got together, they used to sit around a big wine jar and drink out of it. The pigs would come up to join them. Why not? Pigs and men, nature is common to them all and joins them in the fellowship of thirst.

Beginning about the end of the eighth century, there were painters, inspired, I suppose, by such Taoistic feelings, who became famous, or notorious, for their impulsive nature. Chang Tsao, whose pine trees were extraordinary, sometimes painted with his fingers or his whole hand. But he was a master of the brush—or the brushes, as he demonstrated. "He took two brushes in his hands and used them simultaneously, painting with the one a dead and the other a live branch. The vital spirit *(ch'i)* of the tree burst out through mist and haze, its forcefulness defied wind and rain. . . . The live branches were fresh with the sap of spring, the dead ones withered under autumn's blight." An older painter asked Chang who had taught him to spread ink with worn-down brushes or bare hands. Externally, Chang answered, he had learned from nature, but internally he had followed the promptings of his own inspiration. The old man was humbled and decided to give up painting.

Wang Hsia, called Wang Mo, or "Ink Wang," was slightly older than Chang. His pines, stones, and landscapes were made in the bold "splashed ink" style, in which the dark washes were not built up over the light ones, but laid down first. Out of drunken impulsiveness, he soaked his long hair in a pail of ink and dashed the ink onto the silk, to make mist-streaked landscapes. When he died, in 803 or 804, his coffin was found to be so light that people said that his vitality had transfigured him away.

Toward the end of the ninth century, there was Sun Wei, whose brushwork was wild, strange, and saturated with an indescribably strong life-breath. Yet his work was also refined, at least in pines, stones, and bamboos.

Shih K'o, of the mid-tenth century, also had an extremely strong life-breath. As time went on, he became more and more eccentric, uninhibited, and careless of rules. He enjoyed shocking people with satirical rhymes and grotesque caricatures. For example, he drew the officials of the Water Palace with crabs and fishes hanging from their belts.

Between the ninth and tenth centuries, such painters came to be designated by the term *i*, meaning uninhibited or unrestrained. One old theorist explains that to paint in the uninhibited way is difficult and praiseworthy. "Those who follow it," he says, "are not skilled in the use of compasses and square for making circles and squares. They despise refinement and variegated coloring and draw the forms quite sketchy; but they grasp the natural spontaneously. This is not like expressing ideas in a formal manner. The style is therefore called uninhibited."

In spite of the last sentence, it is not known to what

extent the term *i* referred to a particular style of painting. It always emphasized vigor and freedom. Whether the name of a style or simply a value, it was surely an extreme, and critics were divided on the rank of the "uninhibited" painters. Some refused to rank them at all. To judge by existing paintings, not everything that the Chinese critics considered bold seems so to us. The reason may be that we are unable to see the boldness for what it once was, or that the bold originals have been replaced by more timid imitations.

The Search for Inspiration and Longevity

At any rate, the desire to be spontaneous and, of course, inspired was strong even among the conservative artists. Some just waited for inspiration, some invited it, and some did their best to stimulate it.

Ku K'ai-chih is said to have waited for it at the top of a pavilion. Kuo Hsi may be said to have invited it. He would wait until he was inclined to paint, and then, his son tells us,

He would seat himself by a bright window, put his desk in order, burn incense to his right and left, and place good brushes and excellent ink beside him; then he would wash his hands and rinse his inkwell, as if to receive an important guest, thereby calming his spirit and composing his thoughts. Not until then did he begin to paint. Does not this illustrate what he meant by not daring to face one's work thoughtlessly? . . . From beginning to end he worked as if he were guarding himself against a strong enemy.

To arouse the life-breath, artists watched mountains and clouds. As they walked in the mountains and the light changed and the mist grew thicker or thinner, they began to breathe in rhythm with the world's breath. Music, too, could serve, or anything that moved strikingly—a rhythmically rowed boat, a pair of fighting snakes, a dancer. Once, General P'ei Min offered Wu Tao-tzu gold and silk if he would paint him a picture. Wu refused the payment and asked for the general's sword-dance instead. As the general danced, Wu could see his life-breath come and go, and his brushwork became more penetrating than ever, and he finished with quick, godlike intensity.

Taoism taught more complicated techniques for spontaneity, and because spontaneity, the force of life, was supposed to ensure a good long life, they were techniques for longevity as well. The ideal was to be or become a *hsien*, a fabulous "mountain man," who lived out his several hundred years on the earth, moving on, above, or inside it with perfect freedom, enjoying the company of *hsien* or better, and in the end rising to heaven on a ray of sunlight, the back of a dragon, or some other interstellar vehicle.

Hsien, one came to know, were superlatively light. To become light, one had to give up gross foods and live on the more refined, like pine resin and magical fungi. Gentleness, too, and modesty made one more spiritual. Breathing exercises were known to help, for it was supposed possible to learn to live on air, the purest and lightest of foods, and even to guard oneself from contamination by breathing only the air inside one. It was also supposed that an elixir of life could be compounded. Cinnabar, or mercuric sulphide, was a necessary ingredient of this elixir. As a result, when we now read of the conduct of its Taoist users, we can hardly distinguish between the symptoms of mercury poisoning, the symptoms of Taoistic freedom, and such eccentricities as need no chemical or philosophical explanation. Apart from the elixir, there was a sexual technique to lengthen life. It was designed to force a man's semen back up the spinal column, to the spot in the brain where the male and female elements unite and the semen is transformed into life-elixir.

There was hope, it seemed. The great eighth-century poet, Li Po, who needed it, studied Taoist secrets and searched for plants and stones that might prolong his life. A romantic poet, a drunkard, and a Taoist, he is assigned three traditional deaths, a romantic one by drowning as he tried to embrace the moon in the water, an official one from excessive drinking, and a Taoist one by dolphin-back to the sky.

Su Tung-p'o (1036–1101) was another poet-alchemist and drug-compounder. Because he influenced the theory and practice of painting, his name will come up again. As a humane official, he did what he could to relieve the suffering of the peasants. As a Taoist, he searched for completeness and immortality. He trained himself to breathe in and out in a certain rhythm; he meditated in order to get rid of disturbing thoughts; and he tried to direct the wise fire of his heart downward, toward the waters, as he thought them, of animal desire.

The aim of these techniques might coincide with that of art. The arts of Tao gave the concentration and detachment needed for calligraphy and bamboo painting. Tao, the Way, could also be found in brushwork. Art in harmony with nature might itself be a means to long life. The painter and theoretician, Tung Ch'i-ch'ang (1555–1636), quoted the following words to express a view already old:

> The Tao of painting is to hold the whole universe in your hand. There will be nothing before your eyes which is not filled with life, and therefore painters who have not grasped it often become very old. But those who paint in a very detailed manner make themselves servants of Nature and impair their longevity, because such a manner adds nothing to the power of life. . . . Huang Kung-wang became ninety years old and still had a face as fresh as that of a boy. Mi Yu-jen at the age of eighty showed no fading of his bright soul; he died without illness. They were nourished by the vapors and clouds of their paintings.

Taoistic exercises were hard to keep up. It was much easier to look for inspiration in the wine-jar. Li Po and Su Tung-p'o, finding Taoism insufficient, added wine. The calligrapher Huang T'ing-chien, a good friend of Su, was convinced by experience that he could not do his best unless he drank. He said:

> When I was staying in the Hall of Happy Thought of the K'ai-yüan temple I often sat looking at the streams and mountains, at the same time practicing grass-writing, for which they seemed to give some inspiration, whereas Tien Chang-shih and Kuang-seng relied on wine as a stimulant to reach the wonderful. For fifteen years I abstained from wine, and though I tried my best to make good, my tools were not sharpened, the

44

brush was often feeble and stumbling. It seemed indeed that my writing was not so good as when I was drunk. . . .

Tung-p'o . . . was very fond of wine, but could not support more than four or five cups. This was enough to make him absolutely drunk, and without taking leave or saying thanks he would fall asleep and begin snoring through his nose. After a while he would wake up and start writing like a storm-wind, and although the writing was done in a jokingly playful manner, it was very expressive. Truly he was one of the divine Immortals, none of the present-day masters of the brush could compete with him.

In a Drunken
World

Su Tung-p'o is said to have drunk with some moderation. But the distance between his kind of moderation and the excesses of others was not very great. Whatever the truth, in my own mind it is hard to separate Chinese poetry from the smell of alcohol. It would be useless to enumerate all the good poets who used wine, as a Buddhist uses meditation, to forget the world. Juan Chi (210–263) went on a sixty-day drunk to evade his own marriage. Hsieh Ling-yün, though a devout Buddhist, used to sit drunk and semi-naked in public. T'ao Yüan-ming, known also as T'ao Ch'ien, spurned immortality recipes and substituted wine, though much of the drunkenness in his poems may be only poetic. Wang Chi (590?–644), another Taoist, found T'ao Ch'ien's attitudes congenial. Drink, he said, is no elixir of life; but how could he bear to stay sober alone in a drunken world? A near-contemporary, Wang P'o (648–675) got the name Belly-Draft, because his poems seemed to have been drafted in his belly while he lay in drunken sleep. Li Po, though not really up to his boast of emptying three hundred cups in a single round, continually expresses his desire to stay drunk and never wake up. The official history tells how he was brought from the tavern to the palace, doused with water, and set to improvising verse. The Emperor was delighted with his genius. But once, while drunk in the palace, Li wanted his shoes removed and ordered a powerful courtier to perform this menial task, and so, politics overruling poetry, Li was exiled.

One final, extended example, perhaps typical and surely sad, will finish the list. It is the example of Po Chü-i, another poet, like Su Tung-p'o, with a social conscience. In his forties, he was already mourning his grey hairs and anticipating death with wine. Long after, when he had already retired from office, he wrote a description of his life that he seems to have meant to be wistfully humorous. This is the gist of it:

For thirty years he had been an official. Then, on the verge of old age, he had settled with his family on a modest estate. Because of his love for wine, lute playing, and poetry, most of the connoisseurs of wine, amateurs of the lute, and composers of poetry came to visit him. When it snowed or the moon came out and a sympathetic friend was there, he offered him a cup of wine. Then he would open the box with his poems. When sated with wine, he would play the lute or order his servants to sing or play. He would ride through the countryside with a lute, a cushion, a few books of poetry, and some flagons of wine.

Ten years passed in this way. During this time he wrote over a thousand poems and prose poems and drank several thousand gallons of wine. Now his wife, children, brothers, and nephews all criticize him. If pressed, he answers that his pleasures are, after all, relatively harmless. He leads his children and younger brothers down to the cellar and sits with them around a big jar of wine. He sighs deeply, compares himself unfavorably with the ancients, and recalls all he has to be thankful for. He asks his children and brothers, if he now abandons all he loves, how will he spend his old age? So he sings, laughs, drinks, and sings again.

Having taken several cupfuls, he gets drunk and loses consciousness. After a while, he comes to. As soon as he comes to, he again begins to sing. Singing and drunkenness follow one another, forming a continuous circle. This allows him to consider his times and his own existence to be like a dream, and riches and honors like a cloud. The sky is his canopy, the earth his mat, a hundred years are only the wink of an eye to him.

46

Always happy and carefree, he does not see old age as it approaches. That is what the ancients called keeping one's naturalness intact. That is why he gave himself the surname of the writer who intoxicated himself with singing.

In the third year of K'ai-ch'eng (838 A.D.) he was sixty-seven years old. His beard was all white, half of his hair had fallen out, two of his teeth were missing. But his ardor for drinking and singing was not yet slaked.

In China, such a withdrawal was often given a political explanation. Po witnessed a savage struggle for power between the scholar-officials and the Emperor's eunuchs. Waley, his biographer, supposes that he kept representing himself as a decrepit old drunkard in order to be left in peace. But if Po was playing a role, he had had some experience in it—the theme appears much earlier in his writing and is repeated after his retirement from office. A suspicion of alcoholism may be added to the suspicion of politics. His drinking must have been sadder than he said, even if it did have its moments of gaiety. Like the poet Yeats, hoping that though he die old he might seem "a foolish passionate man," Po asks if the retirement rules bar him from singing mad songs or dancing drunkenly. The fear of death arouses the passion for life, and the drunken poet wavers, singing, between the two.

Craftsmen, Professionals, and Amateurs

Although we have considered the attitudes and emotions of Chinese artists, we have so far neglected the distinction, which was to them essential, between craftsmen, professionals, and amateurs. The amateurs, I think, are the most interesting to us; but because they defined themselves by contrast with the others, I will describe these others briefly, especially as they existed in the eleventh and twelfth centuries, when the ideology of the amateurs came to be expressed as such.

The craftsmen, we know, were looked down on. Their numbers were swelled by peasants, escaping misery, who flooded into the cities. Because their numbers were large, their wages were low; but guilds saved them from unregulated competition. Their skill could be exquisite. Collectively, they were masters of all the styles of painting in China. They were considered only craftsmen, not because of any technical deficiency, but because of the attitudes of their customers toward them, and of themselves toward art. But they have had some, at least unconscious, revenge on their artist-kin. Experts say that pictures attributed to well-known artists, the Emperor Hui-tsung, for instance, and those in his entourage, may often have been the work of simple craftsmen. These craftsmen must have been responsible for a large part of the revealed and unrevealed forgeries that make Chinese painting such a challenge to the expert.

I do not know if there was a clear dividing line between the higher kind of craftsman and the lower kind of professional. I suppose that the more a man had had of the scholar-official's education, the less likely he was to be identified as merely a craftsman. Both craftsmen and professionals were kept by officials, landowners, and princes, who, like ancient Romans, advertised their importance by the number of their attendants.

The height of professional success was formal recognition by the Emperor, that is, the granting of the rank of Academician. By the time of the Sung Dynasty, which began in the year 960, there was an established Academy of Painting. By the beginning of the twelfth century, in Hui-tsung's reign, entrance into the Academy was by competitive examination.

Hui-tsung, himself a painter, supervised his Academy of Painting closely. Its members were organized into different ranks, those of Painter-in-Attendance, Painter-in-Waiting, and Scholar of Art. All got regular salaries. Some of them were put on night duty: "A Painter-in-Attendance capable of doing miscellaneous paintings was on service every night in the Jui-ssu hall, to be ready to meet any unexpected call."

Members of the Academy of Painting had to work "in agreement with the rules," in a manner, that is, neither "careless" nor "independent." When a palace fresco dis-

48

pleased the Emperor, he had it plastered over and renewed his instructions to the painter. Like those of seventeenth-century France, the Court artists of China must have struck the more independent artists as dogmatic and submissive. (See Plate IX.)

The more independent, the scholars and scholar-officials to whom art was primarily a means of self-expression, wanted to be the opposites of the craftsmen and professionals. They argued that art and money could not mix, that art could not be measured in terms of money. One of the amateurs, a friend of Su Tung-p'o, said, "The prices of old writings and paintings should not be discussed. Scholars do not like to acquire such things for money; they prefer to exchange them between themselves, which is a more refined way of acquisition." Another of Su's friends claimed that only an amateur was free to be original. "The artisan-painter," he said, "makes his work salable by his skillful craftsmanship; by giving pleasure to the vulgar people of his time, he hopes to make his pictures easier to take. He is afraid only that the world will reject his pictures as different."

Strange as it may seem, the amateurs wanted their pictures to look unskilled. Skill or brilliance, they thought, was for the moneymakers, and they substituted "blandness" (p'ing-tan) and "awkwardness" (cho). They preferred not to please, but to express, not to glitter, but to reveal. They would have appreciated the phrase of the French poet Verlaine, "Take eloquence and wring its neck."

Su Tung-p'o and his friends developed the views of the spontaneous, "uninhibited" painters into an ideology, by which I mean a consistent justification of their art. Their ideology was in part a transfer of the values of calligraphy to painting, or the insistence that calligraphy and painting were the same art. Calligraphers, of course, could not justify themselves by claiming that the words they drew with their brushes resembled something external. Instead, with the uninhibited painters, they thought of their brushwork as exhibiting their own, internal vigor, sincerity, spontaneity, and structure. Su Tung-p'o was therefore able to say that whoever discussed painting in terms of likeness was only a child.

49

This view of art remained moralistic. It was a compromise between Buddhism, which was opposed to men's attachment to the things of this world, and Confucianism, which had always been practical. According to the compromise, which was Neo-Confucianism, men should remain emotionally attached, but not disturbed by their attachment. They should not "fix their minds" on things, but "rest their thought" on them innocently. "Resting one's thought" allowed one to feel as unassertive as a Taoist, as dispassionate as a Buddhist, and as social and practical as a Confucian. It allowed one, that is, to be thoroughly Chinese.

The Art
of Calligraphy

The theory of Sun Tung-p'o and his friends, and the Neo-Confucian ideology that both imitated and resisted it, make a natural preface to a discussion of calligraphy. Calligraphy has so far been mentioned only in passing. The Chinese, however, usually regard it as superior to painting, or as a more essential, purer art. To them, the fourth-century calligrapher, Wang Hsi-chih, is as great as Beethoven to us. The clear April day his brush celebrated on silk-cocoon paper is still one of the great moments of Chinese art. It was the moment a Chinese artist dreams of, in which tradition becomes wholly personal and power and spontaneity are perfectly joined.

In stressing his spontaneity, a Chinese calligrapher may speak as if he were an ungoverned natural force. Su Tung-p'o thinks of his writing as a kind of river. On level ground, he says, it flows calmly, a thousand *li*—over three hundred miles—a day. When it reaches mountains and rocks, it winds around them. It cannot be defined or circumscribed: it flows when it must, and stops when it must.

Even at its most impulsive, the flow of Chinese characters cannot be anarchic. Even when it is the drastic, sinuous abbreviation called "great grass writing," which Su wrote best when he was drunk, the word is assumed to remain

50

true to itself. In principle, its old ideal form remains the same.

The Chinese calligrapher has learned that every stroke of his brush should have "bone," which is strength, and "sinew," which is little, but not too little, "flesh." Each character, he has learned, must stand firmly. The elements of a character should not be crowded or loose; and a deadening internal symmetry should also be avoided. Some of the characters are held together by a strong vertical stroke, others by a frame into which the remaining elements are inserted. Elements of a character may "concede" politely to one another, or one of them may dominate and the others concede. Some, like the members of a family, are sheltered under a rooflike stroke, and some are embraced or enfolded by others.

According to an accepted enumeration, there are eighty-four rules of calligraphic composition. They will not be repeated here. It is enough to note the care with which calligraphy was analyzed, and the subordination of everything to life-breath. As in painting, the artist loved and feared the gathering of tension and its sudden release. Now, he felt, the life gathered in his mind, tensed his arm, flowed down to his wrist, and entered the brush; and now the brush, a poised hawk, plunged down and left a black swoop of words.

Anyone can see that Chinese calligraphy is individual. A traditional book of instructions says:

The first lesson the novice should learn is to look attentively at the peculiar traits of each style. For works of the same style by different artists usually show marked divergences and different pieces done by the same artist are by no means identical. Sometimes strength and sinuosity are coiled in one stroke, sometimes they are coiled forth separately; an apparent smoothness may disguise the bones and sinews, or a burly vigor beat and throb on the surface.

The Chinese were convinced, like modern graphologists, that writing reveals one's character. In an eleventh-century treatise, the author, Kuo Jo-hsü, asks whether calligraphy and painting, "which are done by transferring thoughts and sentiments to silk," do not produce images, seal-impressions of the "innumerable affections, anxieties, and experiences which influence the heart and blend with it." He continues, "The written characters preserve the nobility and the meanness, the successes and adversities of the writer. How could painting and calligraphy but express his high or low life-breath? Painting is in this respect the same as calligraphy. As said by master Yang Hsiung, 'Speech is the sound of the heart (or mind), calligraphy is the painting of the heart; both reveal whether the man is of a superior or of a low kind.'"

Calligraphy is even supposed to mirror the appearance of the writer. Chiang Yee, the contemporary artist, says:

From examples of the Emperor Hui-tsung's writing, executed in the style peculiar to him and termed Slender Gold, we can infer that he was a person of handsome appearance, tall and slim, meticulous as to detail, with a somewhat effeminate temperament; we can even affirm that he was slow and measured of speech. Again, if we study the writing of Mi Fei, the somewhat colloquial English word "tubby" springs to mind as a good description of the artist's general appearance. . . . The writing of Su Tung-p'o suggests to me a man fatter, shorter, more careless in nature than Mi Fei, but broad-minded, vigorous, a great laughter-maker and a great laugher. . . . These are rough judgments only: many finer points could be deduced from more careful study of the written characters.

No wonder that to the Chinese, the answer to the question, "What are you?" was given by calligraphy. In the official examinations, more emphasis was often laid on the calligraphy than on the meaning of the words. The emphasis, however mistaken it might have been in practice, is correct in principle. It anticipates the so-called "projective tests" and the (admittedly uncertain) graphology of our own times. The man who balances his tensions in the characters he draws has reached some expressible balance in himself. Even the belief that calligraphy shows the calligrapher's appearance has some basis in fact. One's gestures belong to one's appearance. Both they and the feeling one has of one's own shape are reflected in the psychophysical gestures of drawing or writing. (See Plate X.)

Ni Tsan,
Ink-Miser

To return from calligraphy to painting, the virtues praised by Su Tung-p'o, and his innerness and spontaneity, found their expression again in Ni Tsan (1310–1374). At first, Ni Tsan had lived the life of a wealthy connoisseur, surrounded by his library and works of art, in a pavilion that breathed an air of remoteness from the world. Later, he gave most of his property away to friends and relatives, and he and his wife wandered along the lakes and rivers of China in a boat. As he had given his property away, he now gave his paintings to anyone who wanted them.

Ni Tsan, who was generally fastidious, and whose scenes were simply composed and bare, was famous for his miserliness in the use of ink. He made almost minimal paintings. His landscapes were empty of human beings, and the traditional pavilion, when it appeared, was empty too. The adjectives that fit him are, "simple, severe, unpretentious, genuine, lonely, chaste, cool." To these can be added the Chinese esthetic terms, "bland" and "awkward."

Ni's defense of his style has a contemporary ring, though his pictures do not look as radical as his words would lead us to expect. For him, he wrote, painting was no more than the pleasure of careless sketching. He wanted to amuse himself, not to paint a realistic image. He remembered how, when rambling about, he had come to a town. The people there asked for his pictures, but when they saw them, they went away scolding and cursing. "What a shame!" exclaimed Ni. "But one cannot scold a eunuch for not growing a beard!"

Ni wanted to be simple and modest. He said:

I-chung always liked my bamboo paintings. I did them simply to express my overflowing heart. My endeavor was not to give an exact representation of their likeness, the profusion or straight position of their branches. I simply brushed and rubbed for a long time. Ordinary people find them like hemp or rushes; I cannot force such people to see that they are bamboos or to take interest in them. Nor do I know what I-chung may find in them.

Once, defending a supposed bamboo he had painted when drunk the night before, Ni said, laughing, that not everybody could achieve a *total* lack of resemblance. This sounds contemporary. But when the great connoisseur, Tung Ch'i-ch'ang, tried to explain Ni Tsan's greatness, he said, "Only Ni Tsan was old-fashioned, simple and natural, he was the only one after the mad Mi [Mi Fei]." Such praise would obviously sound odd if meant for any of the radical modern artists of Europe. In Europe, "simple" and "natural" might be meant as praise, but "old-fashioned" would necessarily be insulting.

Tung's Radical Conservativism

What is odd to us in all this is the need of apparent rebels to attach themselves so firmly to tradition. Tung Ch'i-ch'ang, who was a painter as well as a connoisseur, warned that one should take, not the old masters, but nature as the model. And when there is nothing left to return to, he said, you still have yourself. Yet he and his friends developed a radical distinction between a so-called "Northern" and a so-called "Southern" tradition in painting, with the object of recommending the Southern.

This "Northern" and "Southern" had nothing to do with the geography of painting. The terms were borrowed from the schools of Ch'an Buddhism, which had separated from one another long before. According to the Southern school, which alone survived in China, the highest truth was inexpressible in words. In a stock paradoxical phrase, the truth was to be "stated through non-statement." This attitude, reminiscent of Taoism, was congenial to Su Tung-p'o and the other early amateurs. Therefore the name "Southern" was chosen for the preferred style. It implied: lightly colored or monochrome, simple, natural, free, essential, spiritual, creative. As characterizing a tradition, it could also imply "old-fashioned." "Northern," on the other hand, was a name for everything Tung and his friends disliked.

54

It implied: highly colored, decorative, stiff, external, without life-breath.

Tung and his like did not see any contradiction between learning from nature and from the old masters they chose to revere. Su's or Tung's kind of amateur disliked not only professionalism, but also the intellectual conformity they might have accepted once themselves, and the government they considered to be in the hands of corrupt men. It was therefore useful to them to organize their artistic ancestors into an evil line and a good. To learn from the good ancestors was, precisely, to be free, simple, and close to nature.

It seemed to Tung and his friends that the spirit of the Southern masters could be grasped only if studied closely. To assimilate them one had to copy them in such a way that their values were internalized, that is, the strength of each one captured and his weakness avoided. In Tung's words:

> Someone has said that each one must form his own school, but that is not right. Thus for example, the willow trees should be made after Chao Po-chü, the pine trees after Ma Ho-chih, and the old trees after Li Ch'êng. These are traditional and cannot be altered, and even if they are modified, they will not be very far removed from the original sources. Who can abandon the old methods and create new ones quite independently? Even Ni Tsan came out of Kuo Hsi and Li Ch'êng, though he added softness and refinement. . . . Thus, if one combines in the drawing of the trees the most beautiful points of the old masters and does not waste one's force on stones, the trees will become quite naturally beautiful and moist. Those who nowadays wish to follow the old masters, prepare a volume of copies after their trees to serve as a bag of supplies.

Analytical Exercises and Musical Analogies

To capture the strength of the great artists, Tung and his followers studied techniques and classified them more closely than before. They studied the use of brushes and inks, the varieties of spacing and shape relationship, and the brushstrokes used for texture or modeling. This analytic

55

approach was well adapted to textbooks, which were used increasingly. The textbooks schematized all the elements of painting. They showed, for example, how various artists represented rocks, trees, and birds, and which brushstrokes were suitable for branches, leaves, tree trunks, earth, water, clouds, and clothing. And so the *Mustard Seed Garden Painting Manual*, first published in 1697, lists and illustrates the texture strokes. These, according to their names, resemble spread out hemp fibers, entangled hemp fibers, sesame seeds, big axe cuts, little axe cuts, cloud heads, raindrops, an eddy or whirlpool, the veins of a lotus leaf, lumps of alum, skull bones, wrinkles on a devil's face, raveled rope, brushwood, hair of cattle, and horses' teeth; and also combinations of these.

Detailed instructions like those in the *Mustard Seed Garden*, which encourage painters to assemble imitated rocks, trees, brushstrokes, and styles, appear absurdly mechanical to us now, though they have been known in Europe as well. Whether or not such instructions are good, or to what degree, is surely a matter of history and circumstance, and is in any case to be judged by results rather than theory. But the theoretical justification of the Chinese practice of teaching by analysis and reassembly was quite rational.

According to this theory, a student can learn to perceive well only by assimilating the right gestures. The only way to assimilate the gestures is to copy and recopy. The student copies and recopies the analyzed fragments and brushstrokes and assembles them in the different styles. When these and their rhythms are equally present in his mind and hand, he begins to become able to express himself with their help. He does painting exercises as a student does music exercises. If his instrument is a violin, the music student learns to tune and care for it. He studies, separately, the use of the fingers. He studies vibrato and bowing. He does scales and plays etudes. He studies the styles of different composers and, maybe, those of different violinists.

Chinese painter and European violinist believe that the end is not weakness but strength and individuality, a fusion of old skills in which new, personal emotions can be

expressed. Even in the *Mustard Seed Garden,* sentences
such as these are characteristic:

> In painting pictures, the conception originates from the
> deepest recesses of the heart. . . . To be without method is
> deplorable, but to depend entirely on method is worse. . . .
> The end of all method is to seem to have no method. . . . First,
> however, you must work hard.

Forgery

The musical justification I have given of selective and
expressive copying brings us close to the Chinese practice
of forgery. It was the passion for collecting that made forgery profitable. Forgery, after all, was only misleading repro-
duction, and everyone recognized that the masterpieces of
painting and calligraphy had to be reproduced, that is,
copied exactly. How else could knowledge of the masterpieces be spread among the art-loving public, and how else
could their image survive their own loss or destruction?
When a seventh-century emperor took possession of Wang
Hsi-chih's most famous manuscript, the spring-day celebration we have mentioned, he had his calligraphers make ten
exact copies. It did not matter that Wang Hsi-chih had
himself tried and failed to duplicate it. And so painting
exercises, stylistic tributes, bona fide reproductions, and
plain forgeries became confused with originals. Professionals turned forgery into a family specialty, and at least one
connoisseur, Mi Fei, is said to have kept originals brought
to him for authentication and returned copies.

In time, methods were developed to authenticate paintings. Checklists of items to be examined were made out.
Apart from the style and technique of the painting, such a
checklist might include: the material of the painting; the
artist's inscriptions, signature, and seals; the comments of
earlier connoisseurs written, in the Chinese fashion, on the
painting or its mount, or on attached papers; earlier collectors' seals; and records in old catalogues. But the same
items checked by a collector were checked by the forger
trying to fool him, and each method of authentication pro-

voked a corresponding answer from the forger. (See Plates XI and XII.)

Here, as a description of a simple kind of forgery, are the remarks of a collector of the last dynasty, the Ch'ing:

> If they, the curio dealers, find an old painting they have no particular use for, they cut it down so as to remove the signature, and they write on it the name of some famous Sung or Yüan artist instead. They go even so far as to cut up a very large scroll into three or four smaller ones, writing on each of these auspicious titles. Having in this way assembled a hundred or so of such cut-up paintings, they go and sell them in some other locality. At first I thought that these people engaged in a very risky undertaking indeed. But after a few months I saw them come back with money or with merchandise they had bought elsewhere and which they sold in their home villages; or they purchased with this money some small official rank for themselves. When asked about this they said: "The value of the name of a Sung or Yüan artist ranges within several ounces of gold; thus one scroll will make us gain several times our original outlay." This is something I would never have suspected.

The Chinese have always been rather tolerant of forgery. A perfect imitation was evidence of virtuosity, and the ability to transmit the spirit of an old master was still more. Besides, it was considered impolite to criticize bluntly. Criticism might only express the critic's jealousy, or his desire to lower the value of a picture he wanted for himself. There was also the argument that said, "What he doesn't know won't hurt him," or, in other words, that it was pointless to destroy the illusions of a person too ignorant to know that his picture was a forgery.

The Individualistic
Painters

The last two dynasties of China are named, respectively, Bright and Clear, or, in Chinese, Ming and Ch'ing. The Mings fell in 1644. The period of their decline and fall was one of refined luxury for the upper classes, and of decay and the vitality that flourishes in it. A group of scholar-officials joined in an attempt to reform the government. They lost the power struggle and suffered every punishment up to death and posthumous disgrace. Others of their class lost interest in government service and spent all their time in scholarship and art. Art criticism flourished, and groups of painters worked, consciously and simultaneously, in competing styles. As in our own times, it was possible for an educated man to say that he did not understand a painting.

Because the times were out of joint, some scholars wrote plays and novels rather than the poems that had been considered obligatory. The writing of novels was itself a form of dissipation, but there were scholars dissipated, so to speak, to the second power. These, writes a modern commentator, "found a perverse pleasure in ordure, they wrote the most obscene novels, using the erotic slang of the street, and interspersed that coarse prose with the most elegant erotic verse." There were also scholars who retired to the mountains and the medico-mystical speculation that has been described.

The conquest of the Mings by the Manchus, the founders of the Ch'ing Dynasty, did not give the scholars an easy way out. Difficult as they had found it to love their legitimate rulers, the Mings, they could not easily love the "barbarian" usurpers. Active rebellion was discovered to be fatal. Withdrawal from political life was less dangerous and so was usual.

The Manchus, however, learned to entice scholars into their service. The artists among these tended to follow Tung Ch'i-ch'ang, whose amateur's pride, technical analysis, and radical traditionalism were most persuasive. But the painters who took the old path into the mountains, often to Buddhist or Taoist temples, felt differently. In style and outlook they too were amateurs, but they bowed to no authority, certainly not Tung's. They were defiantly individualistic. One of them, Kung Hsien, was so un-Chinese as to say, "There has been no one before me, and will be no one after me."

One of the best-known of the individualistic painters was the monk Shih-t'ao, also called Tao-chi (1630–1707). He insisted that to imitate the old masters was to be unfaithful to their spirit. His long essay on painting is directed against

59

Tung and the others who respected the past too much. Here are a few freely rendered passages:

It's been said, "The perfect man has no method." That doesn't mean that he has no method, but that he has the perfect one, the method that's no one else's method.

Everything regular has its variations, every method can be changed. If you understand anything regular, you can vary it; if you understand a method, you can change it.

People today don't understand this. They always say, "So-and-so's textures and dots ought to be the basis of art. Landscapes that don't look like so-and-so's won't last. Without so-and-so's cleanness and freshness, his skill's only fun." You think that way and you're the slave of another artist and you can't use him. Even if you keep close to him, you're only eating his leavings. What's the use of that to you?

Somebody says to me, "That artist makes me big, that other one gives me discipline. What school should I belong to? How should I go about things? Who should I imitate? What effects should I try for? What kinds of outlines and textures? What shapes and compositions will make me into an old master and an old master into me?"

Whoever talks like that only knows that there are old masters, but not that there's a me. I'm always me, myself. The beards and eyebrows of the old masters can't grow on my face. You can't stick the old masters' guts into my belly. I say what's in my own guts and wear my own beard and eyebrows. If sometimes I look like some master, it's because he looks like me, not because I've copied him. It's natural to me. Why follow some old master instead of changing him?

I could go on with the story of individualism in Chinese painting, up at least to the eccentricities of the eighteenth century—the use of fingers and fingernails instead of brushes, for example. But I have said enough to show that China, in its own way, bred the kind of artist who wants to stand out and be unique, like the familiar "genius" of the West. Because I think that artists in general, but especially such men, are motivated by pain, I should like to recall the evidence that this was true of the individualistic amateurs of China, beginning with Su Tung-p'o and his friends.

Su himself, though he aims at Buddhist "nonbeing," defends calligraphy as an amusement that helps us to forget:

If, even though it does not achieve non-being, one can enjoy oneself with it for the moment, in order to give a lodging to one's mind, forget the sorrows of one's declining years, then it is a wiser pastime than gambling or chess.

This is Su's testimony on himself. His friend, Mi Fei, testifies that Su's rocks and trees were "queerly tangled, like sorrows coiled up in his breast."

Su once described a friend, a great painter of bamboos, who felt his painting to be not a gift, but a symptom:

In his early years Yü-k'o painted his bamboos wherever he found some pure white silk or good paper. He grasped the brush quickly, brushing and splashing with it quite freely. He simply could not help it. Whoever came to his house grabbed some pictures and carried them away. Yü-k'o did not trouble about them very much.

In later years when he saw people placing brushes and ink-stone on the table, he recoiled and went away. And those who came to ask for pictures waited until the end of the year, but did not obtain anything. When someone asked Yü-k'o about his reasons for this, he replied: "In former years I studied Tao, but could not reach it; I found no peace of mind and could not express it. Therefore I simply went on painting ink-bamboos, expressing my restlessness through them. It was like an illness. Now this illness is cured, nothing more remains to be done."

As far as I can see, Yü-k'o's illness is not yet cured. Is it not possible that it will develop again? I will wait for its development and take him by surprise. While he thinks that he is ill, I can take advantage of his illness—perchance I too may be ill.

Among the individualistic painters of Shih-t'ao's time, there were a number who were at least queer. Chu Ta (Pa-ta Shan-jên), who had become a Buddhist monk, decided one day to stop talking. He put a sign, "Dumb," on his door and forever after held his tongue. But he did not hold his peace, and whenever he picked up his brush to write, he would utter cries like a madman.

Shih-ch'i (K'un-ts'an) was another contemporary who retired from the world. He symbolized his isolation by painting a monk sitting in a tree and looking down. On the painting he wrote:

The problem is to find peace in a world of suffering. You ask why I have come here. I do not know the answer. Here I can live, free from every care, like a bird in its nest. People say that I am a dangerous man, but I answer them, "You are demons."

In a poem written in 1662, Shih-ch'i describes his feelings as he paints a landscape in his cubicle in the mountains. Below there is the harsh world. Somewhere which is nowhere there is Nirvana. Around him there is the mountain range with its life-breath. Under his hands there is the painting, by means of which he is drawn into reality. Shih-ch'i speaks to himself:

Renunciation is too difficult. It is better to be in the mountains and painting them. A diet of fasting and a monk's robe need no money, and now it is four years that he has been painting such paper. Single brushstrokes create nothing one can recognize, but with a thousand, with tens of thousands something comes into existence, a landscape that is nowhere at all in the world. Shih-ch'i feels himself penetrating into the structure of the landscape. He is playing peacefully. Past and future disappear. "I know only the feeling of this one time. I do not care where this sheet of paper will remain."

He finishes the picture and goes out to climb in the mountains. He is happy to see them, he is deeply moved when the clouds rise out of the gorge, and his heart stops when the far-off mountain bells ring. A blast of wind, and the mountains glitter like tigers. Frightened, he moves and his foot strikes against a sharp rock. He only laughs. He wanders back into his room and stands before the picture. He is someone else now, changed in an almost inexpressible way. To get to reality, he says to himself, he no longer has to go through the mountain gate. He says, "I penetrate into the invisible with the ink-moistened tip of a brush."

On a picture painted eight years later, in 1670, Shih-ch'i writes a few lines epitomizing his troubles and his need to paint because of them:

War in its tenth year, ten years' sickness
Extinguished all life and hope.
Youth, long decayed, remained unforgotten.
Mountain and cloud became the painter's vision.

62

Sadness and Detachment

Motivated by such thoughts, Chinese art is often close to depression. The grays and unsaturated colors that are so dominant in amateur painting are meant to be "bland," but they are also sad. The dominance of gray is always sad. In Chinese painting, the gray constitutes mist, which dissolves away the definiteness of things. And as the mist is a wish, the neutrality of its color is a flight from all strong emotion. Everything, in the color sense, is degraded, and only the faceless sage, who regrets and accepts, is left.

Chinese poetry, too, is grayed, and not only by its unwilling Stoicism. There is something in the structure of classical Chinese like the gray of the paintings. I am referring to the impersonality of the language. Although this cannot be sensed in ordinary translations, pronouns are often omitted. Important as it seems to us, the *I* is infrequent. The subject is anyone or everyone, because number, too, is often unstated. Verbs may be omitted, and when used may have no tense. The reader's feeling may be that it is his mind, which moves from noun to noun, that adds the motion, much as his hand unrolls a scroll, while the words are still.

The depersonalizing gray and mist of the painting, and the impersonality of the poetic language combine to give Chinese art a strong sense of detachment. This is increased by the artist's consciousness of tradition and his elaborate self-discipline. The poet notices the historic precedents that are repeated in his own experience, and the artist thinks of the famous picture of which his is a variant. "See how spontaneous I am," the Chinese artist is always saying as he paints a scythe-shaped blade of grass a little higher or lower or more to the left or right than his revered predecessor. Except if he is Ni Tsan, he is so thoroughly the spectator that he always paints himself as such into his landscapes: he watches himself watching.

The detachment of the Chinese artist is an inherent quality of his very nature as such. There are Western writers, Thomas Mann, for one, who believe that the artist is by nature detached. As Mann experienced it, this detach-

63

ment is a painful half-divorce from what one wants to have or live completely. Like Mann, the Chinese artist, split into an observer and an enjoyer, invents techniques to capture the immediacy that continues to elude him somewhat. That is why he so values inspiration in and for itself, and cultivates a dramatic swiftness, cleanness, and flexibility of motion.

The Chinese, then, concentrate on the glittering things that pass because they feel that life is escaping from them. They feel that every moment of pleasure must be paid for in a moment of pain. Listen to the poet, Li Po. "What is the world?" he asks, and answers, "A wayside inn for all living things." "And what is time?" he asks, and answers, "A stranger, travelling through eons." The conclusion is the usual one that "our life is like a dream," and the advice that follows is, "wine." Li Po has such dreams in wine, he says, that he will never tell them to the sober; but because the dream is wild and great, the shock of awakening is hard to bear. Every dream has its end. He imagines himself the enormous legendary bird, the P'eng, which mounts a whirlwind and storms heaven; but even the P'eng's strength, he sighs, is suddenly exhausted.

It is true, it seems, that to be aware of each moment and sensation is to be at least on the verge of sadness. The hand is made to grasp and get things, but the Chinese artist puts it over his heart to feel each separate beat. Chinese art shows that there is something constricting the Chinese character painfully, driving it inward, maybe as the result of too much discipline and fastidiousness. But the art that expresses this constriction and inwardness also defends against it.

3

Historians

THE MEN AND THEIR

INSTITUTIONS

I N some moods, almost everything seems mysterious, in others, clear. When people say, as they automatically do, that the Chinese mind is mysterious, sometimes I agree. But I always deny that it is more so than any hypothetical "mind" of any civilization. Because this book is in the mood of clarity, not mystery, the Chinese mind is assumed to be intelligible. A number of its elements already have been identified. These include: piety toward family and elders; awareness of the social hierarchy; examinations and other trials of potential and actual officials; esthetic sensitivity; formalized discord between convention and spontaneity; and sadness revealed in art, especially the art of "amateurs." Another essential element, which has appeared in the guise of reverence for tradition, can now be made explicit. It is the consciousness of history.

History
and Art

The consciousness of history never left Chinese thought. To the Chinese, as to the Jews, history came near replacing mythology. History furnished its rich materials not only to the Chinese moralist, but to the storyteller, novelist, dramatist, and, less openly, to the poet and painter.

Remember the painter. Remember that he painted ceremonial portraits, antiques, and illustrations of historical events. Remember that he trained and understood himself as the willing or rebellious heir of long artistic traditions, and that he often tried to compile himself out of previous painters. Sometimes he had a realistic ideal. Yao Tsui was a sixth-century example of a realist who wanted to get his characters' clothing just right. The painter's sense of history could be detailed and acute, for there were many antiquarians among Chinese scholars. As an example, take Kuo Jo-hsü, the eleventh-century historian of Chinese painting. The era represented in a painting should, he said, be strictly observed:

Prior to the Three Dynasties, all men went barefoot. With the dynastic age, they began to wear wooden clogs. I Yin made sandals out of grass and gave them the name of *li*. In the Ch'in period they made use of plaited grass in combination with leather. Hsüeh boots were originally an item of Tartar dress, but Prince Ling of Chao liked them, and ruled that the proper footgear for officials in long outer gowns should be black boots. In the reign of Tai Tsung of the T'ang, the palace ladies and attendants were ordered to wear high boots of scarlet brocade. . . . In working out a picture, one should pay careful attention to points such as these.

Now remember the poet. Remember how conscious he was of the themes and techniques of his predecessors. Remember how he sighed that his life was passing so quickly. In a moment of longing, he recalled the great beauties of the past he had read about, in a moment of trouble, the troubles of the heroic scholars of the past. Neglected, he recalled the long-dead poet whose emperor "had cast him off like a snapped stalk." He wrote "poems on history," using historic events to comment on contemporary ones. After visiting an ancient battlefield, where he had picked up an old arrow, he wrote, "In tears, seeker of ancient things, I picked up this broken barb." At an appropriate ancient site, he recalled the historian's moral that a dynasty must perish when the cycle of its life was ended. And he kept writing variations on the writer's eternal hope that "men of a later age" would appreciate him better.

The storytellers and novelists borrowed more, and more directly, from the historians. Some storytellers specialized in historical tales, even those of a brief given period. Stories were set in mock-historical time and provided with mock-documentation and plausibly concrete detail, for facts look like facts; and so we learn, for example, at the beginning of a story that "Miss Li, ennobled with the title 'Lady of Ch'ien-kuo' was once a prostitute in Ch'ang-an. The devotion of her conduct was so remarkable that I," says the teller, "have thought it worth while to record her story." Then, to establish the historical background, he says, "In the T'ien-pao era there was a certain nobleman, Governor of Ch'ang-chou and Lord of Jung-yang, whose name and surname I will omit."

A device of this kind is, of course, universal among story-tellers. The structure of the Chinese stories is also the usual string of episodes, which we might call, for our purposes, the mock-historical chronicle. The Chinese novels often had more complex characters, and they followed the histories more closely and accepted their sadder view that decency is not always rewarded, for history alternates between periods of order and periods of anarchy. Later novelists were able to become more self-sufficient. Because the respectability of novels was in question, their quality could be judged only by comparison with an accepted prose masterpiece. The standard proved to be a history—that is, Ssu-ma Ch'ien's *Records of the Historian*, a work to which we must later return.

Family History

The Chinese, who venerated ancestors and lived in and for families, naturally preserved family histories. Han Suyin, the contemporary writer, describes the historian of her family, known to her as Third Uncle, who kept the family documents and collected, classified, and retold the family traditions, with all his frenzy for exactness and his astonishing memory.

What picture of his family's existence did Third Uncle retain?

All things under heaven have their rise and fall; and these occur beyond our intercession; only resolution and uprightness, virtues bequeathed by our ancestors, can transform ruin into resurgence. That is why a family erects its ancestral sanctuaries, to maintain the veneration due to progenitors and the remembrance of its own humble beginnings. Hence the necessity for filial virtue to accomplish the rites due to the spirits of pred-ecessors; hence forbearance among members of a household, to remember one's responsibilities, to strengthen the clan and the breed, to inspire sacrifice of self for the common good. In these ways our Chou clan, remembering and holding fast to virtue, has risen once again. From the seventh generation, when ancestor Chienhsi entered into the southern province of Kwang-tung (after the Mongol ravages) till the fifteenth generation, when ancestor Mofah moved from thence to Szechuan, these filial rites were followed. Loyal and upright, practicing agricul-ture, and industriously learning, our family held together, in spite of manifold disaster. In the seventeenth generation our ancestor Hsinghua first established himself in Chengtu at the Street Si Fu Nan, where he acquired a piece of land for building. In the eighteenth generation ancestor Chaochung and his younger brothers, on the piece of land, erected a Sanctuary for the veneration of soul tablets, and also built a habitation and dedicated it to the ancestor Hsinghua, calling it the Hsinghua Branch Sanctuary. Here now, at the Branch Sanctu-ary, we offered ritual sacrifice, from generation to generation, continuing until our present twenty-third generation. Thus the family was not parted but remained together, acquiring merit by fulfilling the ideal of five generations under one roof.

On a photograph, taken in 1907, of the surviving mem-bers of this family, one sees three venerable old men in golden monkey-fur gowns. A scroll on the wall reads, "O future generations, see this, and remember to stay united."

Biographies

The oldest known full biographies are the ones in Ssu-ma Ch'ien's history, the date of which is roughly 100 B.C. Biographies were written for many purposes. They were used in family cults and for commemorations, and they made up much of the content of gazetteers and histories, local, regional, or national, unofficial or official.

The scholar-bureaucrats who composed the biographies for the official histories did so in terms of their own fixed conventions. They could revenge themselves on unworthy members of their class, or on enemies such as the Court eunuchs or, at one time, the finance officials, by refusing them biographical notices. Unworthy men might be erased out of history, at least as individuals.

The historian composing the official biography of an important bureaucrat could draw on a number of sources. For the family line, he had the official genealogies, and for positions occupied and for evaluations of merit, he had the record kept by the Board of Civil Office. A section of this same Board prepared an Account of Conduct. In the words of an official history:

The Secretary and Under-Secretary of the Department of Merit Assessments are responsible for . . . Accounts of Conduct. When an official dies they send one to the historians. When a posthumous name is to be granted to an official by the Court of Sacrifices they use this Account of Conduct to decide whether or not it is suitable. When they wish to engrave a stele, they assemble the officials to discuss what is fitting to be written on it and report the outcome to the family of the deceased.

Such accounts might be written by respectful disciples. In any case, an official biography was less the record of a man's personal experiences than of his official career. It began with the initial facts—the man's name, family place, and male ancestor. It then went on to a page or so on his childhood and youth. Here the biographer would praise the mother's virtuous influence and recall her dreams that foretold her son's future. Other signs and prophecies would be recalled. The son, the future great man, was likely to be poor, but virtuous and studious. He was, we may suppose, extraordinarily quick to learn the Classics, to which his character was attuned, and no less extraordinarily retentive.

After these stylized facts or legends came the serious part of the biography, the official record. It began with the man's first considerable success in examinations. The rest was a record of examinations taken, official posts filled, honors granted, and punishments inflicted, and of patrons, collaborators, and friends—in short, of his bureaucratic functions and social roles. The more interesting biographies would have telling quotations and anecdotes that might rise to a succinct eloquence.

Examples may help make this abstract description more clear. They are taken from official biographies of writers of the T'ang Dynasty (618–907). These writers were classified apart, for they had not been great bureaucrats and were therefore considered specialized and rather inferior. Here is a pretty example of the prophecies that could attend the birth of a writer. The one in question was born some time in the 580s. In order not to multiply unfamiliar names, we shall call him "X."

X was born exactly at noon on the fifth day of the fifth month. At that time, several unusual birds with extremely small, five-colored bodies gathered on a tree in the courtyard, drummed their wings in unison, and chirped beautifully. The Director of the Imperial Observatory of Sui . . . had just come to Ch'ing Prefecture and happened to be present. He interpreted the omens as follows: "The fifth month is fire; fire is brightness; brightness is literary splendor. The exact hour of noon means the acme of literary perfection. Then there are birds of five colors, beating their wings and chirping. This boy will surely become a brilliant writer whose fame will spread over the entire world. Since the birds are small, his salary and rank will probably not be high.

Childhood anecdotes were repeated because it was assumed that a man's character, being fixed, could be made out very early. That a writer was "renowned for his filial piety" as a boy meant that his character as an adult would be good. That "he was able to recite stone inscriptions from memory and to reconstitute the arrangement of a chessboard" meant that he would be intellectually brilliant. An adult writer might be praised with the words, "He governed with integrity and strictness," or, for ability to compose literature, with, "He would finish as soon as the brush touched the paper."

It was supposed that the writers of whom we are speaking had weaknesses that prevented their full success as officials. Thus one was said to be "boastful," "gay and extravagant," and partial to "wild hunting." Characteristically, four famous writers of the seventh century are damned with the judgment that although they "possess literary talent, they are unsteady and shallow. Surely they are not made of the stuff required for achieving high rank."

We can see the conventions at work, in their subtle and perhaps inextricable admixture with reality, in the official

72

biography of Li Po, which was finished, for the *New History of T'ang*, in the year 1060. The biography immediately supplies an eminent ancestor and explains the decline of his family from its eminence:

Li Po, surnamed Tai-po, is a descendant in the ninth generation from the emperor Hsing-sheng. His ancestor in the latter part of the Sui Dynasty was for some reason exiled to the west barbarian land; but the family escaped and returned in the beginning of the Shen-lung era. They sojourned in Pa-hsi.

Now comes his mother's prophetic dream:

At the time of Po's birth his mother dreamed of the planet of Chang-keng, and because of this he was named after the star.

Now his precocity is recognized:

At ten years of age he was versed in "The Odes" and "The History."

A little further comes the mention of the first important official to recognize his abilities:

Su Ting became Governor of I-chou. On seeing Po, he wondered and said, "This lad is a genius, he is brilliant and singular. If a little more learning be added, he may be compared with Hsiang-ju [the great Han poet]." (See Plate XIII.)

Now comes the tale of his shifting fortunes, in part that of the shifting fortunes of his patrons. For example:

Ling, Prince of Yung, called him and made him a subordinate of his staff. When Ling started war, Po fled to Peng-tse. But with the fall of Ling, Po was sentenced to death. . . . He received pardon. . . . Sung Jo-ssu . . . placed Po on his general staff. But before long he resigned. When Li Yang-ping became governor of Tan-tu, Po went to live with him.

In the meanwhile, there have been anecdotes on Po's drinking and his spontaneous, exquisite poems. Last come the stories that show that his genius was suitably recognized. One important action came too late:

Emperor Tai Tsung ascended the throne, and he summoned Po to take the office of the censor of the court; but Po was then dead. His years were sixty and a little more.

From the Chinese standpoint, this was far from the end. Therefore the significance of his posthumous honors:

In the beginning of the Yuan-ho era [806–820], Fan Chuan-cheng, Inspector of Hsuan-che, performed rites at his grave, and forbade woodcutting at the place. He sought for descendants of his. There were only two granddaughters, who were married and were wives of peasants, but who carried with them an air of refinement. They wept and said, "Our grandfather wanted the Green Hill; but he is buried at the East Base, that is not his true wish." Whereupon Chuan-cheng made a reburial and erected two monuments.

The great, but drunken and frivolous Li Po is treated biographically with less respect than a statesman (see Plate XIV). Lu Chih (754–805), who fled a rebellion with the Emperor and became his secretary and drafter of state papers, may be contrasted with Li Po. The only likeness was the effortless swiftness with which he worked:

The whole empire was in turmoil and beset with difficulties. Affairs of state piled up, mobilization and exactions had to be carried out far and near. The policies of state had to follow up innumerable lines of action. Each day several tens of edicts had to be promulgated. All these came from Lu Chih's hand. Wielding the brush and holding the paper he completed his drafts in an instant, and yet he never needed to rewrite anything. Although it appeared that he had given no thought to the matter in hand, when it was completed there was never any detail of the matter which had not been covered, and it was exactly what was needed for the circumstances. The clerks making copies of these documents had no rest, while his colleagues just sat and sighed with folded arms, unable to assist in any way.

Lastly, to show what personal ideals might be, we give an example of the eulogy. This eulogy is of Chu Hsi (1130–1200), the great statesman-philosopher, of whom we shall speak again. Written by his son-in-law and disciple, it depicts the model of a Neo-Confucian sage, exceptional in his learning, intelligence, and self-discipline, and in his ability to reconcile withdrawal from public life with participation in it, that is to say, sagehood with politics. The eulogy is as follows:

74

As regards his personal appearance, his facial features were dignified, his language was to the point, his movements were steady and respectful, and his thinking was straight. He rose before dawn, and wearing a robe, a hat and square shoes, every day worshipped his ancestors in the family temple, and paid respect to the sages of old. Then he went into his study where his books, tables and things he needed were arranged in a very orderly fashion. At the dining table the dishes and chop-sticks had to be laid out according to a prescribed plan. When he felt tired, he would take a rest by closing his eyes sitting bolt upright. After resting, he took a short walk. He retired at midnight. When awakened during the night, he sat up, well covered, and waited until dawn. His features and movements were in conformity with habits which never changed, whether in youth or in his old age, whether in midsummer or in midwinter, whether at leisure or in haste. In his private life, he showed the utmost filial piety towards his parents, and love towards the younger generation. Since he showed such respect and affection, there was harmony in his family. When offering sacrifices, he carefully observed form, even to the minutest detail, and if anything went wrong he worried the rest of the day, but if all went well he was happy. At funerals he expressed sorrow, wore correct mourning clothes, and partook of the foods that were properly served. He was polite to all visitors who called on him. To relatives, however distant, he showed love. To neighbors, however humble, he showed respect. He never overlooked any detail of what should be done on the occasion of others' birthdays, weddings, periods of mourning, distress, etc. In regard to his personal comforts, he wore just enough clothing to keep himself warm, ate just enough to prevent starvation, and lived in a house just well enough constructed to protect him from the wind and the rain. Surroundings which other people might have found unbearable Chu Hsi accepted with complete satisfaction. In matters of public service, his district program and his proposals to the Emperor were based on a policy which was properly orientated and dignified. Though he was unfortunate in his political career and was unable to carry out publicly his *Tao* [Way], he was able, in retirement, to illuminate his *Tao* so brilliantly that it will enlighten coming generations for a thousand years.

The Forms
and Purposes
of History

During the early, formative period of Chinese thought, there were men, later grouped under the heading of Legalists, who insisted that the imitation of the past would be socially destructive. They used the argument we have heard from Tao-chi, but for political purposes. To imitate their independent predecessors, they said, was to be false to their spirit. Not one of the idealized early dynasties, they said, had been imitative: "The Chou dynasty did not imitate the Shang dynasty, nor did the Hsia dynasty imitate the period of Yü (i.e., the Emperor Shun); the three dynasties encountered different circumstances, but all three succeeded in attaining supremacy."

In one of the Legalist books we find this idea supported by a story. A farmer was once tilling his field when a hare ran violently into a tree nearby and broke its neck and died. The man then left his plow and waited at the tree, hoping to get another hare in the same way. But he never did, and the people ridiculed him. The moral was that "the sage does not aim at practicing antiquity, and does not model himself upon what is considered to be permanently correct. He discusses the affairs of his own age and prepares for them accordingly."

By and large, this attitude of independence with respect to history was repudiated by the Chinese. They recalled the mercilessness of the Legalists, and they learned, no doubt, that they could always find the precedents they wanted, and so they came to prefer the Confucian dependence upon precedent. Ignorance of history was a crippling blindness, they thought. In the words of a rather old source, "No gentleman of high standing will be found among those who repudiate the past in discussing the present, and no gentleman of wisdom will be found among those who are ignorant of the past and are easy-going in their achievements. Even though one may be completely virtuous in his own conduct, if he repudiates the past he will be a mediocre man."

76

The origins of Chinese historiography are obscure. Because the word *shih*, "historian" (and "history"), also meant "scribe," we can make the assumption, which is in any case the plausible one, that the historians were descended from the record-keepers, who dealt with the ritual calendar, with predictions by astrological and other means, with state correspondence, and with Court annals.

The first historical work written by an identifiable author is the *Shih chi*, the earlier-mentioned *Records of the Historian*. Its author, Ssu-ma Ch'ien (145?–90?B.C.), who incorporated his father's work into his own, strikes us as extraordinarily ambitious. Not only were his interests varied, and not only did he begin as far back as history or legend could reach, but he included all the peoples and regions known to the Chinese. This was a new historical comprehensiveness, which matched the comprehensiveness of a great bureaucratic state. It made his history difficult to organize. His solution was to divide it into five parts: a chronological account of the rulers of China; chronological tables of the empire's feudal states; special treatises; annals of the local, predynastic states; and "Memoirs," consisting mostly of biographies. Ssu-ma's became the typical Chinese solution. Simplified, it was to divide history three ways— into chronological "Basic Annals," treatises on special subjects, and classified biographies.

Ssu-ma's chronological account or Basic Annals, giving the main events in the reigns of the emperors and dynasties, provided the thread of time on which everything could be located. His Treatises, eight in number, took up subjects that would have interrupted the earlier, political sequence. They were on rites, music, the pitch-pipes, the calendar, astronomy, sacrifices, the Yellow River and canals, and economics. The stress is on the ritual matters that interested the Chinese Court. This now odd interest is balanced for us by the interest in economics, which is easier for us to appreciate.

Ssu-ma's history closed with the section called "Memoirs." The biographies it contained were meant, as usual in China, as moral illustrations. In the words of Ssu-ma's miniature preface, "Upholding righteousness, masterful and sure, not allowing themselves to miss their opportunities, they made a name for themselves in the world. Of such men I made the 'Seventy Memoirs.' "

Ssu-ma's classifications of the biographies are interesting in themselves. The Biographies of the Reasonable Officials, who "upheld the law and carried out their duties in a reasonable fashion" and "did not boast of their accomplishments," precede the Biographies of the Harsh Officials, who used "the sternest and most severe treatment." The contrast is meant to satirize the harsh officials, the type that Ssu-ma had met so often in his own lifetime. There was also criticism implicit in the Biographies of the Wandering Knights, benevolent men who acted on the principle of "saving others in distress, helping those who cannot help themselves." The Biographies of the Emperor's Male Favorites were of "those who served the ruler and succeeded in delighting his ears and eyes," but not only "through the power of lust and love." The most modern note is struck in the Biographies of the Money-Makers, who earned their biographical notices because they were able, "without interfering with the government or hindering the people's activities," to get rich "by making the right moves at the right time."

Appropriately, the Memoirs ended with Ssu-ma Ch'ien's autobiography. It will be cited later.

From the time of Ssu-ma Ch'ien's masterpiece, Chinese history grew to enormous proportions. No one I know of has tried to estimate the total number of historical works. Even the types that were recognized were so many that I am almost afraid to enumerate them. However, to reinforce what I am saying, I will repeat an accepted eighteenth-century list: 1—Standard Histories, having the standard form of Annals, Treatises, and Biographies, and officially sanctioned by the government; 2—Annals, chronologically arranged; 3—Narratives from Beginning to End, topically arranged for a given period; 4—Separate Histories, usually in standard history form but without government sanction; 5—Miscellaneous Histories, usually short and on more or less contemporary events; 6—Decrees, Mandates, Memorials, and Recommendations, that is, collections of state papers and of advice presented to the throne; 7—Biographical Memoirs, containing only biographies, whether official or not; 8—Historical Excerpts, mainly from the standard histories; 9—Contemporaneous Records, of states contemporaneous with the recognized dynasties; 10—Regulation of Time, works on chronology; 11—Geography, historical geographies of the empire and numerous local histories; 12—Functions and Offices, on the evolution of official ranks and functions; 13—Treatises on Government, describing the machinery of government systematically and historically; 14—Catalogues, that is, library catalogues and works on inscriptions; 15—Historical Criticism, critical comments by historians on other historians and sometimes on themselves.

The list can be forgotten. It is more important to remember the purpose for which most history was written and read. Whatever its incidental interest, most history was written by salaried bureaucrats for the benefit of other, actual or potential, bureaucrats. This explains the objectivity that was aimed at, as well as the limit of this objectivity. The limit was the need to accept directives from above and to set one's patron and government in a favorable light. The objectivity lay in the need to be accurate, by which I mean, to quote the basic documents, and do so correctly, to get just right who had said what to whom and what had happened afterward. This objectivity, because it dealt with the whole of official human nature, could give a whole narrow education. Precedents were, of course, of great importance, and collected regulations could serve to amuse scrupulous officials after hours. There was a perpetual issuing, gathering, preserving, and digesting of documents, for they were needed for the activity of governing, and they were the testimonies from which to learn the subtleties of bureaucratic behavior. At its least attractive, the history that came of all this was a string of amputated citations joined together by clichés.

The Progressive
Construction of
Standard Histories

Standard Histories were constructed in painstaking stages. Like the tips of pyramids, they rested on a great, spreading base—of documents, not of stone. Below, at the very base, were two sets of records, the one called Diaries of Activity and Repose, and the other, Records of Current Government. As will be explained, these were very detailed. Out of the Diaries and selected government reports, so-called Daily Records were compiled. Together with other official reports, all the records named above were sifted, cut, and edited into a Veritable Record. From this was produced either a National History, of the current dynasty, or a Standard History, of the preceding one. The Standard History was made public, as were collections of official statutes. But all the other, very extensive records—the Diaries of Activity and Repose, the Records of Current Government, the Daily Records, and the Veritable Record—were kept secret. There were only two copies of each, one official, and one secondary. However any of the materials might be revised, the unrevised versions were kept during the lifetime of a dynasty, so that an emperor could always decide what revision of the truth he preferred to hand on to the next dynasty.

The convention was that the history of a dynasty should be finally compiled by the dynasty that succeeded it. This convention was used to legitimize the new regime, to allow a show of generosity toward the preceding one, and to detach the scholar-bureaucrats from their old loyalty. A loyal scholar, like a filial son, was duty-bound to preserve the memory of the dynasty to which he had been attached; but in proving his loyalty, he would in turn become attached to his new employers. New dynasties tried to cajole loyalist scholars into their service. The degree of their success varied, but in the long run the advantage lay with the government, the great traditional employer of the scholar-officials.

80

Truth and Concealment

The preceding remarks on history have been flavored with cynicism. But there was more in Chinese objectivity than the requirements of the official who wants his documents uncorrupted. There was also the courage of the historian imbued with his moral standards and, in his own fashion, in love with the truth.

The Chinese historians took courage from incidents recorded in their own histories, this one, for example:

The year 642, Summer, 4th month, The Emperor T'ai-tsung spoke to the Imperial Censor, Ch'u Sui-liang, and said, "Since you, Sir, are in charge of the Diaries of Action and Repose, may I see what you have written?" Sui-liang replied, "The historiographers record the words and deeds of the ruler of men, noting down all that is good and bad, in hopes that the ruler will not dare to do evil. But it is unheard of that the ruler himself should see what is written." The Emperor said, "If I do something that is not good, do you then record it?" Sui-liang replied, "My office is to wield the brush. How could I dare not to record it?" The Gentleman of the Yellow Gate, Liu Chi, added, "Even if Sui-liang failed to record it, everyone else in the empire would," to which the Emperor replied, "True."

Another such famous story was recorded in these words:

The year 839, Winter, 10th month. The Emperor Wen-tsung went to the Official in Charge of the Diaries of Action and Repose, Wei Mo, picked up his notes and began looking at them. Wei Mo objected and said, "The Diaries of Action and Repose record both good and bad in order to warn and admonish the ruler of men. Your Majesty should only strive to do good. It is not necessary that Your Majesty see the records." The Emperor said, "Once before I looked at them." "That," replied Wei Mo, "was the fault of the official in charge of history at that time. If Your Majesty were to examine the records personally, the historiographers would be forced to distort or alter their accounts. Then how could we expect later ages to put any faith in them?" With this the Emperor desisted.

81

During the T'ang Dynasty, as these incidents show, the Emperor still respected the objectivity of the Diaries, on the principle that his passion to be recorded as a good ruler would help keep him so. But even when he stayed away from the Diaries, he received and approved other historical materials. If his approval was emphatic, he might reward the historians who had prepared it. Furthermore, the writing of any history that involved him was supervised by one of his own chief ministers. In fact, the old principle of truthful recording was opposed to another old one, of appropriate concealment. One subtle way of concealing with generosity and yet respecting the truth was to omit a man's minor faults in his biography while recording them elsewhere. In the later dynasties, the historian's personal criticism came to seem unfitting to the Standard Histories. The irritations of criticism were replaced by tranquilizing eulogies. The official attitude was expressed by one of the compilers of the Ming History, who said, "Official compilation of history is different from private writing. In private writing it is permissible to use one's personal views as a basis. When a history is compiled by imperial order, it is necessary to integrate the collective, impartial judgment of the empire. One should not trust his own opinion and indulge in criticism."

Proposals and Institutions to Preserve Truth

During the Ming Dynasty, there was a long period during which the Diaries of Activity and Repose were not kept. The result, said a critic, was that the national historiography failed its task as never before:

> The Diaries of Activity and Repose are missing. Thus the compilers of the Veritable Records had no material upon which they could rely, and therefore they were not in a position to write. As to national disgraces and imperial faults, there was reason for evasiveness and they did not dare to write. But the worst of all was that those in charge of the writing had their

private sympathies and aversions therein; thus even if there was material to rely upon and nothing to evade they did not wish to write; and therefore if they wrote, it did not correspond to the facts.

The keeping of the Diaries was resumed in 1575, in answer to a memorial from a statesman who shared the sensitivity toward the truth of the criticism I have just cited. But his proposals also testify to the experience of the bureaucrat, this time in the service of a passion for objectivity. I therefore repeat a few of his proposals, which were later embodied in government regulations, as paraphrased in the source I have used:

Among the different duties of the historiographical officials, the recording of the Diaries of Activity and Repose was the most important one. One official, changed daily, was to record the Diaries at each Imperial audience and also to write down the complete texts of all Imperial edicts, proclamations, commands, patents, etc., as well as of the memorials of the Grand Secretariat. After secret consultations with the emperor, the Grand Secretaries should at once give the necessary information to the official in charge of the Diaries. Furthermore, six elderly and learned historiographical officials should be ordered to record regularly the memorials presented to the Throne by each of the Six Boards. These officials should be free of all other duties and only be responsible for the exact recording of the memorials of their respective boards.

Since these records would only provide the material for the later compilation of the Veritable Records, exactness was of greater importance than a refined and beautiful manner of writing. Imperial utterances must be recorded literally and should not be put into literary style. In the texts of the memorials only insignificant matters of minor importance might be left out; only passages difficult to understand owing to unclear wording might be slightly improved. Otherwise all texts were to be recorded without alteration. Causal connections and temporal sequence were to be made clearly evident. The content must not be changed or modified in any circumstances. The historiography officials were strictly prohibited from expressing their own opinions or "praise and blame."

Prescriptions concerning the safekeeping of the records. At the end of each month the manuscripts written by the historiographical officials were to be bound into seven volumes, one comprising the Diaries of Activity and Repose and six others the materials from the Six Boards. On the cover of each volume, year and month, as well as the name or names of the historiographical official or officials responsible, were to be noted. The complete volumes were to be sent to the Grand Secretariat for inspection and be sealed there in a small chest. At the end of a year, the volumes of that period were to be taken out of the small chests in the presence of the historiographical officials and all twelve together re-sealed in a larger chest. After that sealing, the volumes should not be touched again.

In spite of the criticism we have repeated of Ming historiography, the Mings too exercised what would seem to us excessive care. As an example, take the work of the distinguished committee that was ordered, in 1373, to compile the Daily Records of the Great Ming:

The work was carried through under supervision in a special part of the Imperial Palace strictly closed to the outer world. Early in the morning the members of the committee went together to their working-room; there they got food and left only in the evening to retire together to their dormitory, likewise carefully separated from the outside world. During the period of nearly nine months until the completion of the work, none of the collaborators was permitted to get into touch with people from the outside. The whole enterprise was kept strictly secret in order to prevent interested people from trying to influence the compilers. These were required to base their work only on the written material available. This was in accordance with regulations issued by the Emperor, which also stated that after its completion the work was to be inspected by the Emperor and safeguarded in a metal chest, a copy being deposited in the Imperial Library. . . . The preface written by the officials directing the compilation states clearly that the Daily Records serve as basic material for the later compilation of the Veritable Records. The rigorous secrecy observed again shows the importance placed on recording the governmental actions of the Emperor accurately and without inference for transmission to later generations.

The Veritable Records were treated with the same care. Occasionally, as has been said, they might be officially revised. During the Ming era, there was even an instance in which a Grand Secretary stole and destroyed pages that mentioned him unfavorably. But the precautions against such transgressions were elaborate:

84

Two manuscript copies of the Veritable Records were presented to the Emperor in an exactly prescribed official ceremony. Thereupon the original copy was put under seal in the Grand Secretariat—later in the Imperial Historical Archives— and was not allowed to be taken out again. It provided the fundamental source for the compilation of the official history by later generations. The duplicate copy was for reference, being at the disposal of the Emperor, of the Grand Secretaries, and of the historiographical officials, and was likewise deposited in the Grand Secretariat. In order to guarantee secrecy all drafts and preliminary copies were burnt at a specified place in the interior of the palace in the presence of all officials who had participated in the compilation.

Interlude: Chinese, Greek, and Moslem Historians Compared

The Chinese historians will stand out more clearly if they are compared with the non-Chinese. I will omit our own, familiar historians from the comparison, and include those of the other civilizations in which historiography was highly developed, the Greco-Roman and the Moslem.

Chinese historians write as men who are filling a particular function, Greek and Roman historians as individuals. Less subordinate to their tradition, less subordinate in general, the Greeks and Romans do not confine their personal remarks to little prefaces and epilogues. They have no elaborate historiographical forms or rules to keep. Each one is, without concealment, himself.

Herodotus, the first Greek historian we really know, is closer to a Chinese novelist than to a Chinese historian. He discovers moral lessons in history—one, that ambition fails if it goes beyond the proper human bounds, and another, that free men have the advantage over the unfree. He is, however, a storyteller rather than a moralist. His history is designed to be recited, and he neither wants nor dares to be dull. Truth is not allowed to dominate pleasure.

There are Greek historians with more Chinese aims. Plutarch, half a millennium after Herodotus, has them, though he too loves a good story. His expressed aim is moral, and he teaches morality through the exemplary lives of good and evil men of different types. And the Roman historian, Tacitus, says in words that might be borrowed from China, "I believe it is the main function of history to rescue merit from oblivion, and to hold before evil words and evil deeds the terror of posterity's censure. . . . Few men have the intelligence to discern the good from the bad, the expedient from the harmful; most have to learn these lessons from the experience of others."

Unlike the Chinese, Greek historians do not often speak in conventionally pious words. Herodotus values freedom because it feels good to be free. In this sense he is egotistical, and a proper Confucian, while he would listen to Herodotus with interest, would condemn him or consign his tales to the morally "empty" category of fiction.

Unlike Herodotus and like the Chinese, Thucydides prefers truth to attractiveness. Like them, he believed that "in the order of things" the future will resemble the past and a knowledge of the past can clarify the future. But the lessons he learns are less like the pious ones of the Confucians, which dominated Chinese thought, and more like the harsh, theoretically abhorrent ones of the Legalists. Humans, to him, are motivated by honor, fear, and profit. When the chance arises, they are naturally aggressive. There is nothing here of Chinese harmony, no more than of Hebraic, Christian, or Moslem obedience to God. When the Spartans claim they want to save Greece, he tells us that really they are afraid of the growing power of Athens. In a famous dialogue, the Athenians tell the inhabitants of Melos, "You must act with realism on the basis of what we both really think, for we both alike know that in human reckoning the question of justice only enters where there is equal power to enforce it, and that the powerful exact what they can and the weak grant what they must." But power cannot be held automatically, and therefore Thucydides follows the themes of fear as against enthusiasm and of calculating intelligence as against blind rashness. When Athens fails and falls, it is, he implies, because of human nature, because there are so few leaders with character and intelligence, and because the crowd is irrational. He is somewhat enigmatic and distinctly modern.

I. This detail of a painting shows a birthday or anniversary party in the country house of an obviously important family. The seated elders are being offered gifts and respectful greetings by at least two generations of their descendants. The detail is from a 33-foot scroll called *Spring Festival on the River.* Now in The Metropolitan Museum of Art, the scroll is a 16th-century variation of a 12th-century original painted at the order of the Emperor Hui Tsung. (Photograph courtesy of The Metropolitan Museum of Art, New York; Fletcher Fund, 1947. The A. W. Bahr Collection.)

II. A 19th-century picture of the members of a family drowning an "unfilial" son in a well.

III. The village teacher has fallen asleep, with entertaining consequences. The painting, from the Tien-lai-ko Collection, is attributed to the Sung Period (960–1279 A.D.). (Photograph courtesy of Lin Tsiu-sen, *Meisterwerke Chinesischer Tuschzeichnungen,* de Clivo Press, Zurich.)

IV. A connoisseur showing his pictures to a friend. From one of a large number of illustrative paintings made by the artist Wu Yu in the 1880's. (Photograph courtesy of Instituto Italiano per il ed Estremo Oriente publishers of R. Van Gulik: *Chinese Pictorial Art.*)

V.

VI.

A sad pair of illustrations. Illustration V is an engraving, made in 1786, of "The Great Fountains" of an imperial palace founded by K'ang-hsi and later enlarged by Ch'ien-lung. Illustration VI is a photograph of the ethereal terrace, fountains, and pond vanishing into rubble. (Illustrations courtesy of Madame R. Osvald Sirén from *Gardens of China* by R. Osvald Sirén.)

A photograph (VII) of a pine tree in Shantung, China, compared with a section of a scroll (VIII), *Landscape* by Hsia Kuei, active about 1200. The painting, now in the Nelson Gallery of Art and Atkins Museum, Kansas City, proves to be more realistic than might be suspected by someone not familiar with Chinese trees and landscapes. (The photograph ''Pine on T'aishan'' is courtesy of Walter Hochstadter. The Hsia Kuei *Landscape* is courtesy of the Nelson Gallery-Atkins Museum, Kansas City, Missouri.)

IX. Part of a 16th-century scroll by Ch'iu Ying—a careful painting of a court painter making a careful portrait of an empress or imperial concubine. A Chinese text says that "Ch'iu's paintings were beautiful and elegant, full of delicate and graceful detail. The brushwork was so refined that the pictures looked as if they had been carved in jade. . . . He was particularly skilled in painting gentlemen and ladies; they were all brilliantly colored and looked alive." His style influenced that of the Japanese print-makers. (Painting in the Collection of the National Palace Museum, Taipei, Taiwan, Republic of China. Photograph courtesy of Editions d'Art Albert Skira, Geneva, Switzerland; from J. Cahill, *Chinese Painting*.)

X. A poem written on silk by the Emperor Hui-tsung. "Hui-tsung developed a completely personal style of calligraphy, which Chinese scholars have described as 'delicate metal (or gold) script,' that exactly mirrors the emperor's artistic and sensitive nature. . . . The emperor was intent on increasing the elegance and refinement of his hand and he therefore developed peculiarities of technique which are not usually permissible. Long straight strokes are often finished with a sharp angle instead of the more customary thickening. . . . Despite these rather self-conscious effects, Hui-tsung's script bespeaks a noble mind with a stern introverted nature." (Courtesy of Oldbourne Press, reprinted from W. Speiser, R. Goepper, and J. Fribourg: *Chinese Art*.)

XI. This *Landscape in the Style of Ni Tsan,* now in the Princeton Art Museum, was painted by Shih-t'ao. It is dated 1697. The diagonal path, which pulls the spectator's eye into the picture, and the mountain set directly behind the trees, are said to create a visual unity impossible to Ni Tsan, three hundred and twenty-five years earlier. "The lines no longer serve to render objects formally, as the objects seem to be made into some impressionistically blurred vision of freely running and whirling lines and areas of ink-washes. . . . This painting is, indeed, an admirable example of the late Ming and early Ch'ing ideal of *'hsieh-i'* or 'idea-writing.' The picture may be said to have been 'written' rather than painted. Thus, apart from the obvious pictorial motifs of trees, rocks and a lone pavilion, its sole link with Ni Tsan is an expressive one." (Reprinted from Wen Fong, *The Problem of Forgeries in Chinese Paintings, Artibus Asiae,* Ascona, Switzerland, by permission of *Artibus Asiae.*)

倪詩老人若瓜偶言

此畫之妙以無遠神也

微茫其枯索寒儉處

空靈清潤之氣冷逸人

轉隨注幽乎自然而一段

倪高畫畫如浪谿沙磤石隨

XII. This version of the *Landscape in the Style of Ni Tsan,* in the Abe Collection, Osaka, is said to be no more than a superficially successful freehand copy. Perhaps it may be called a forgery. It would be futile to make a close comparison of "original" and "forgery" by means of small reproductions. It may be pointed out, however, that the calligraphy has shrunk away from the painting and become essential to its balance, and that the mountain peak seems to have been painted in after the trees and to hang, so-to-speak, self-consciously above them. The brush-strokes are said to have become mechanical and the ink-washes dead blobs. Shih-t'ao, for all his freedom, always recalled the natural structures from which he began. These the "copyist" appears to forget; he relates less to nature and more to the painting he is imitating and turns natural forms and depths into a cold, two-dimensional pattern. Or so the critic says. To judge from the reproductions, I think he is right, at least in his distinction of better painting from worse. (See Wen Fong's study referred to in the caption to the previous illustration. Reprinted courtesy of *Artibus Asiae.*)

XIII. Li Po, by the 13th-century Ch'an painter, Liang K'ai. Not, of course, an actual, but an ideal portrait of Li Po as "brilliant" and "singular." The attempt to suggest the poet's force of life with the help of a loosely enveloping mantle reminds me somewhat of Rodin's Balzac. The technique is basically *p'o mo,* which is to say, "splashed ink" or "spilled ink." (Reprinted courtesy of Lund Humphries Publishers Ltd. from O. Sirén, *Chinese Painting, Leading Masters and Principles,* Vol. III, London, Lund Humphries.)

XIV. Li Po, by an unknown painter, prob ably of the Ming period. This is a mor literal Chinese gentleman, seeing h visions in a wine-colored mist. (Reprinte courtesy of Ernest Benn Limited, from I Binyon, *The George Eumorfopoulos Co lection Catalogue of the Chinese, Korear and Siamese Paintings,* London, Erne: Benn, Ltd.)

宋蘇漢臣

XV. "A Group of Children at Play" (probably 17-18th century, Ch'ing Dynasty), by an unknown artist. The children are playing at Buddhism. One of the boys is acting the priest, another holding an image on a tray, and one of the girls is playing at praying. I take this picture as a reminiscence of a playful childhood; but there are strong hints of discipline, in the gravity of the children, in the slow, grave, rigid technique, and in the subject—for the content of their game will become their social duty. (Photograph courtesy of Yale University Art Gallery, The Hobart and Edward Small Moore Memorial Collection, gift of Mrs. William H. Moore.)

XVI. The great astronomical clock, as reconstructed by John Christiansen, water-wheel at the center, celestial globe above it, armillary sphere on top, and, at the side, the revolving figures that marked the time. (Reprinted courtesy of Dr. Needham and Cambridge University Press, from J. Needham, *Clerks and Craftsmen in China,* London, Cambridge University Press.)

XVII. A section from a large scroll by Ch'ên Jung, dated 1244, in the Museum of Fine Arts, Boston. The dragon, turbulent, terrific, and unpredictable, is the embodiment of *ch'i*. A contemporary of Ch'ên Jung writes: "In his dragon-paintings he has grasped the idea of cosmic transformations. He makes clouds by splashing the ink *(p'o mo).* He forms vapors by spitting water. When he is very drunk he shouts loudly, takes off his cap and soaks it in the ink and then smears and rubs with it. After, he finishes the picture with his brush. The dragons ascend and descend, they bend down in order to exhale the vapors, they look around full of rage, they squat down and clasp the rocks with their claws. . . . Could it be that he holds a gift from Heaven in his bosom?" (O. Sirén, *Chinese Painting,* II, p. 150). (Photograph reprinted courtesy of Lund Humphries Publishers Limited, from O. Sirén, *Chinese Painting, Leading Masters and Principles,* Vol. III, London, Lund Humphries.)

Unlike the Chinese, Greek historians are often unable to assume that there is only one civilization, their own. Herodotus has a respectful interest in the Persians and Egyptians. Polybius tries to write universal history, though this is in the end dominated, he thinks, by Rome. Diodorus Siculus begins with Egypt and ends with Caesar. I mention him not for his quality, which is mediocre, but for his aim, to be universal. He approves of the historians "who have made it their ambition to bring the whole of mankind, which is one in mutual affinity, if divided in space and time, into a single system and under one comprehensive view."

When we turn to the Moslem historians, we find that they, like and unlike the Chinese, subordinate themselves to tradition. Like, because of the subordination itself, unlike, because this subordination is to Allah, the willful, unfathomable director of history, and to his revealed Word. To him and his will, all bears witness. The notion of witnessing is itself a key to the historian's technique. He aims to trace witnesses, judge their character, and evaluate and join their testimonies.

Conquest, trade, and travel teach the Moslem historians what the Chinese do not know, that there are worlds outside their own and civilizations other than theirs. At their best, they try to be impartial historians of humanity. Al-Biruni (d. 1048) shows a remarkable combination of such impartiality with a historian's industriousness. In prefacing his book on India, he explains, "I did not spare either trouble or money in collecting Sanskrit books from places where I supposed they were likely to be found, and in procuring for myself, from very remote places, Hindu scholars who understand them and are able to teach me." Out of respect for direct witness, he condemns what earlier Moslems have written on Hindu religious doctrines. He says, "Everything which exists on the subject in our literature is secondhand information which has been copied from others, a farrago of materials never sifted by the sieve of the critical method." As for his own aim, he says, "This book is not a polemical one. My book is nothing but a simple historical record of facts. I shall place before the reader the theories of the Hindus exactly as they are, and I shall mention in connection with them similar theories of the Greeks in order to show the relationship existing between them."

Although objectivity is high in the best of the Moslem historians, and although they may be extremely industrious, their ability to synthesize is weaker than the Greeks'. They tend to string events out one after another. The underlying explanations are generally superficial and forgotten in favor of picturesquely edifying anecdotes. To this generalization, Ibn Khaldun (1332–1406) is a notable exception.

The Chinese historians, we have learned, identify history with morality as closely as the orthodox Moslems, Jews, or Christians. To a Chinese, however, the forces that direct history and destroy immoral dynasties are less personal, less ascribable to a God with an individual will, and more simply natural. Like all of nature, history, to the Chinese, is the play of forces that always change and always remain in balance. Some of the Greeks and Romans, influenced by Stoicism, had a vaguely similar cyclic theory.

Through its underlying generalizations and its moral precepts and preceptors, Chinese history joins Chinese philosophy very intimately. This connection between history and philosophy is far closer than in Greece, where the two may be considered opposites, and closer than in Moslem countries, where philosophy, though religious, is modeled on Greek abstractions. The Chinese see history in a way both impersonal and humanistic. There is a not-quite-secular interpenetration of nature, man, and morality of a sort much less usual in the West.

We have reviewed the evidence that shows how extraordinarily institutionalized, documented, and copious Chinese history has been. Its concept of rigor has been higher than that of any age before our own, and its concept of history by teamwork has only recently arisen again. Its unit is usually the artificial dynastic one, and its standard often success rationalized as morality. Its ideals of objectivity and critical analysis are explicit and developed in functional detail. In spite of the protests we shall hear from some Chinese historians, it tends to remain deeply stereotyped. In this it is the same as most history everywhere, but its institutionalization and rigor make the persistence of the stereotype more

88

evident. It is, so to speak, the same kind of mountain of evidence, but being much higher, it is seen from much further. Because it is intended as a record, and because there is so much of it, its language is compact. It has a triple aim: to be useful, in Chinese precedent-style; to be gravely archival; and to be properly eternal. It therefore does not have the expansively pictorial qualities we find elsewhere. It is made not of word-pictures but chains of documents. It smells more of the bureaucrat's files than of life, but is not invariably the worse for that.

Six Historians

1. *Ssu-ma Ch'ien* (145?–90? B.C.)

Granted that Chinese history is relatively anonymous, official, and stereotyped, it also has exceptions, its historiographical individuals, rebels, prophets, and thinkers. Six of these exceptions will be discussed here, the first of whom is Ssu-ma Ch'ien, the first of Chinese historians.

Ssu-ma Ch'ien inherited his position and his sense of duty from his father, the Grand Historian, Ssu-ma T'an. It is hard not to be moved by the words, recorded by the son, in which the father hands on his historian's role, which has become what he cares about most, before and after death. These are the words:

The Grand Historian grasped my hand and said, weeping, "Our ancestors were Grand Historians for the house of Chou. From the most ancient times they were eminent and renowned when in the days of Yü and Hsia they were in charge of astronomical affairs. In later ages our family declined. Will this tradition end with me? If you in turn become Grand Historian, you must continue the work of our ancestors. Now the Son of Heaven, following the tradition of a thousand years, will perform the Feng sacrifice on Mount T'ai. But I shall not be able to be present. Such indeed is my fate! After I die, you must become Grand Historian. When you become Grand Historian, you must not forget what I have desired to expound and write. . . . I have been Grand Historian, and yet I have failed to set forth a record of all the enlightened rulers and wise lords, the faithful ministers and gentlemen who were ready to die for duty. I am fearful that the historical materials will be neglected and lost. You must remember and think of this!"

I bowed my head and wept, saying, "I, your son, am ignorant and unworthy, but I shall endeavor to set forth in full the reports of antiquity which have come down from our ancestors. I shall not dare to be remiss!"

The image that has been drawn of the Chinese historian is that of a man who made history out of books and documents. But Ssu-ma Ch'ien amplified these with personal experience. When he wrote, for example, on the Yellow River and on the canals, he had seen them with his own eyes. He tells us this briefly, beginning with the formula that introduces personal remarks:

The Grand Historian remarks: I have climbed Mount Lu in the south to observe the courses which Emperor Yü opened up for the nine tributaries of the Yangtze. From there I journeyed to K'uai-chi and Tai-hung and, ascending the heights of Ku-su, looked out over the Five Lakes. In the east I have visited the confluence of the Yellow and Lo rivers, Ta-p'ei, and the Backward-flowing River, and have traveled along the waterways of the Huai, Ssu, Chi, T'a, and Lo rivers. In the west I have seen Mount Min and the Li escarpment in the province of Shu, and I have journeyed through the north from Lung-men to So-fang. How tremendous are the benefits brought by these bodies of water, and how terrible the damages! I was among those who carried bundles of brushwood on their backs to stem the break at Hsüan-fang and, deeply moved by the song of Hu-tzu, I made this treatise on the Yellow River and the canals.

Ssu-ma held the usual Chinese idea of the cycles of nature, and his problem, as a historian, was to make them visible, especially in the confused beginnings of history. The idea was, at bottom, a magical naturalism. Applied to history, it was that the sage, the ancestor of the dynasty, accumulated merit, *te*, which was also power. This powerful merit or meritorious power was transmitted by him to his heirs and assured them, as it had assured him, of power and prosperity. But, like the sea, where it had once flowed, it began to ebb. A virtuous ruler still could stem the tide and restore the power, but if he did not appear in time, the power would ebb all away, and another dynasty, its power fresh, would destroy its predecessor. It is interesting to note that this idea of *te* resembles Machiavelli's idea of *virtù*.

In spite of the dominance of the cyclical ideology in Ssu-ma Ch'ien, he does not seem to have a very consistent point of view. His sympathies vary. Sometimes the will of heaven decides things, and sometimes men decide, but why sometimes the one and sometimes the other Ssu-ma does not try to tell us. His vacillation may be caused by the need to use "veiled" because dangerous words. Yet his vacillation is also his sincerity, which cannot make conventional justice of what he has seen:

> Even in more recent times we see that men whose deeds are immoral and who constantly violate the laws and prohibitions end their lives in luxury and wealth and their blessings pass down to their heirs without end. And there are others who carefully choose the spot where they shall place each footstep, who "speak out only when it is time to speak," who "walk on no bypaths and expend no anger on what is not upright and just," and yet, in numbers too great to be reckoned, they meet with misfortune and disaster. I find myself in much perplexity. Is this so-called "Way of Heaven" right or wrong?

Compare this perplexity with the story Ssu-ma told of the Empress Dowager Lü and her son, Emperor Hui the Filial. Emperor Hui was "by nature weak and soft-hearted," while Empress Lü "was a woman of very strong will." The third character in the story, Lady Ch'i, had been a favorite of the preceding emperor, Hui's father. Empress Lü hated Lady Ch'i and had her imprisoned. The rest of the cruel story is as Ssu-ma tells it:

> Empress Lü later cut off Lady Ch'i's hands and feet, plucked out her eyes, burned her ears, gave her a potion to drink which made her dumb, and had her thrown into the privy, calling her the "human pig" [she was kept in the swine's pit below the privy]. After a few days, she sent for Emperor Hui and showed him the "human pig." Staring at her, he asked who the person was, and only then did he realize that it was Lady Ch'i. Thereupon he wept so bitterly that he grew ill and for over a year could not leave his bed. He sent a messenger to report to his mother, "No human being could have done such a deed as this! Since I am your son, I will never be fit to rule the

empire." From this time on Emperor Hui gave himself up each day to drink and no longer took part in affairs of state, so that his illness grew worse.*

Empress Lü seems an almost legendary monster, but the reaction of her son makes the story psychologically convincing. A normally consistent moral theory would have required the Empress to be punished, at least by fate. By what effort of objectivity or realism was Ssu-ma able to give a favorable report on her reign?

The Grand Historian remarks: In the reign of Emperor Hui and Empress Lü, the common people succeeded in putting behind them the sufferings of the age of the Warring States and ruler and subject alike sought rest in surcease of action [from the vast projects and strict regimentation of the previous dynasty]. Therefore Emperor Hui sat with folded hands and unruffled garments and Empress Lü, though a woman ruling in the manner of an emperor, conducted the business of government without ever leaving her private chambers, and the world was at peace. Punishments were seldom meted out and evildoers grew rare, while the people applied themselves to the tasks of farming, and food and clothing became abundant.

It was no doubt not only Ssu-ma's objectivity that made his final judgment favorable. Private and state morality need not be identical, the *te* of the dynasty was still at its zenith, and the reaction to an oppressively active government was to prefer a peacefully inactive one. But there was still reason for a historian to be perplexed, and Ssu-ma Ch'ien, who was honest, made this clear.

One of Ssu-ma's responses was a sympathy, Chinese enough but not conventionally Confucian, for the "knights errant," the nonconformists who lived as they cared, like Robin Hoods, rescuing people from the callous arm of the law. These men were not only courageous, but put justice above even family loyalty. Where the Confucians believed in love and duty by degree of relationship, they believed in an identical morality for everyone. Where the Confucians believed in the golden mean and in "deferring," they were extreme, unyielding, and vengeful. Stories were told of how

* Compare, for their inhumanity, some of the stories in Tacitus, *e.g.* *Annals*, Book XIV, on Nero's relations with his mother, Agrippina.

they had committed suicide rather than betray a trust. "They always meant what they said," Ssu-ma repeats, "always accomplished what they set out to do, and always fulfilled their promises."

Here, now, is Ssu-ma hedging somewhat, praising the punctilious gentlemen, but in order to be allowed to praise the rebellious "knights":

Men who stick fast to their doctrines and observe every minute principle of duty, though it means spending all their lives alone in the world, can hardly be discussed in the same breath with those who lower the tone of their discourse to suit the vulgar, bob along with the current of the times, and thereby acquire a glorious name. Yet among the knights of the common people there are men who are fair in their dealings and true to their promises, who will risk death for others without a thought for their own safety, and who are praised for their righteousness a thousand miles around. So they have their good points, too; they do not simply strive to get ahead at any price. Therefore when people find themselves in trouble they turn to these men for help and entrust their lives to them.

Perhaps Ssu-ma's deepest moral is that of the artist and poet. There is no consistent reward for virtue or punishment for evil. The reward lies less in life itself than in the history by means of which it is relived. To write history is to join the men, past, present, and future, who contemplate the truth. Even the truth that the world is fickle is itself, like virtue, steady.

Before I leave Ssu-ma Ch'ien, I should like to compare him briefly with Tacitus. Both were men with official religious duties, but neither was especially reverent. Ssu-ma was an official recorder or interpreter of omens, whereas Tacitus was a member of the "college" that kept the Sibylline oracles and supervised foreign cults. More important to the comparison, both historians were dealing with large, complex, newly established empires, which succeeded in maintaining themselves against the pressure of barbarian nomads. Both were primarily interested in politics, which, in both empires, ran to intrigue, poisoning, sex, and ruthlessness—that is the way they saw it from where they stood, at the center of their respective worlds. Both had a high, moral conception of the way men ought to act politically, and both saw their periods as in moral and political decline. Both were themselves active in politics, both were intelligent and conscientious, and both were somber. There are so many likenesses between them, that it should be rewarding to study them together carefully.

The Chinese continued to read Ssu-ma Ch'ien with interest and love. It was said in his praise that he had worked out a new, useful arrangement of historical materials, had put down facts without evasion, was logically clear, and had a pure style. But most Chinese also learned to object to his unconventional respect for merchants and defence of outlaw knights. He was accused of Taoistic bias and of too much love for the strange, "in contradiction to the spirit of the Classics." But by now his faults have turned to virtues.

2. *Liu Chih-chi* (661–721 A.D.)

At the age of eleven, Liu was already a passionate student of history. With the help of borrowed and hired books, he gave himself a fairly extensive education in history while still an adolescent. He was ambitious to compare sources and write a genuinely critical history of China. After he had worked on an anthology of religious texts for the Empress, he was assigned to the writing of official history. He found bureaucratic methods hard to bear, and tried, but failed, to resign from the History Office. He was a co-worker on a number of Veritable Records. His career was interrupted by exile, the result of his attempt to shield his son from a criminal accusation. He died soon after having been sent into exile.

Liu's *Generalities on History*, finished in the year 710, is the first historiographical treatise written in China. The autobiography it contains expresses his dissatisfaction with the History Office:

In all that I wrote I wished to carry out my long-cherished principles but my fellow workers and the high officials in charge of the work were completely out of sympathy with this. All that I wrote and edited was vulgar and of low standing. Although in my own eyes I felt that I was bending and conforming, I still incurred much ill-will from the History Officers.

94

. . . I was filled with gloomy discontent and solitary resentment. If indeed I should have nowhere to confide my feelings but keep them to myself unexpressed, I was afraid that after my death I would be unknown. So I withdrew and privately wrote the *Generalities on History* to make my mind known.

More concretely, Liu complained that so many people had to give their approval to the work that nothing was ever decided; that the officials in charge gave contradictory instructions; that the history could not be kept secret and was interfered with by people criticized in it; that government documents were now too hard for historians to get at; and that bureaucratic inefficiency too often left the historians with nothing to do.

Liu became notorious because of the sections of his *Generalities* entitled "Suspicions about Antiquity" and "Doubts about the Classics." Every text, he said, should be examined to see if it is internally consistent, consistent with other, better accepted texts, and inherently probable in itself. Using such criteria, and without excess reverence, he examined even the works attributed to Confucius.

Among other subjects dealt with in Liu's *Generalities*, there are many that remain of interest. He suggested that monographs be added on cities and on clans. He opposed the inclusion of documents that contained no real information. He surveyed the judgments of historians by historians. He distinguished between literary and historical talent. And he took up the eternal problem of historians: the writing of a truthful history.

3. *Ssu-ma Kuang* (1019–1086)
4. *Cheng Ch'iao* (1108–1166)
5. *Ma Tuan-lin* (1250?–1325)

These three historians had in common the desire to write continuous history, not broken up into the usual, artificial dynastic units. The great early example of continuity was the work of Ssu-ma Ch'ien. He had respected what we should call the organic unity of history, and what the Chinese called "meeting and joining."

Ssu-ma Kuang and his collaborators wrote a chronological history of China covering more than 1,300 years. Their accomplishment was to fuse into a single clear, objective narrative, hundreds of sources, from the standard official histories and records to geographical works, private biographies, inscriptions, and poems. The very range of the sources made it especially important to decide which version of an event to accept. The choice, Ssu-ma Kuang insisted, had to be justified. He therefore gave his collaborators these instructions for notes to accompany the text and explain the choice that had been made:

First note the rejected versions thus, "Such and such a book says . . . such and such a book says . . ." Comment, "Such and such a book has such and such evidence," or if there is no such evidence, then reason it out according to the circumstances of the case. . . . [Then say] "Now we follow such and such a book as established." If there is no means of deciding between true and false, then say, "Now we retain both versions." Veritable Records and Official Histories are not necessarily always to be relied on, miscellaneous histories and anecdotes are not necessarily without foundation. Make your own choice by your own scrutiny.

Cheng Ch'iao defended his partisanship of "meeting and joining" with the words:

The many rivers run each a separate course, but all must meet in the sea; only thus may the land be spared the evil of inundation. The myriad states have each their different ways, but all must join the greater community which is China; only then may the outlying areas escape the ills of stagnation. Great is this principle of meeting and joining.

The most explicit defense is given by Ma Tuan-lin, who regards political, but not institutional, history as divisible into dynasties. The laws and institutions of the different dynasties are interrelated:

Thus from the Ch'in and the Han down to the T'ang and the Sung, the regulations concerning rites, music, warfare, and punishments, the system for taxation and selection of officials, even the changes and elaborations in bureaucratic title or the developments and alternations in geography, did not suddenly spring into being as something unique for each period. Thus the court etiquette and governmental system of the Han was based upon regulations of the Ch'in; the military and tax sys-

96

tems of the T'ang were based upon Chou statutes. Therefore to understand the reasons for the gradual growth and relative importance of institutions in each period, you must make a comprehensive and comparative study of them from their beginning to their ends and in this way try to grasp their development.

6. *Chang Hsüeh-ch'eng* (1738–1801)

Chang was a genius who early recognized himself as one. Though relatively obscure when alive, he is now regarded as an outstanding historical thinker, the greatest among the Chinese of his time. His thought, concentrated in a number of essays and letters, is still stimulating. Those familiar with Hegel, Burckhardt, or the Pragmatists will recognize the affinities between their thought and his.

As a child, Chang wrote, he was sickly and stupid. His life was filled with difficulties. He was poverty-stricken at times. He rose up the examination ladder with difficulty too—he took the examinations for the degree of Recommended Men three times before he passed them, and he did not become a Metropolitan Graduate before the age of forty. In old age, he was, it is said, red-nosed, warty, deaf, stammering, and subject to constant headaches.

Chang once described even his early study of history, which he loved with fanatical zeal, as restricted by an inability to concentrate:

Since I was young, I have been by nature inclined to the study of history. But because historical books are so very numerous, I had to pawn my clothing to buy the sixteen or seventeen Histories from Ssu-ma Ch'ien to Ou-yang Hsiu and Sung Ch'i. My power of comprehension was limited, and I would often absent-mindedly lose the thread of thought; with red ink I would go over and over the text four or five times before I began to get the idea, and still I wasn't able to comprehend all the phrasing or the technical details.

But though dissatisfied with himself, Chang was also dissatisfied with the histories he read:

I thought that the twenty-one [Standard] Histories had impurities of form and exhibited many faults in content, and so I wanted to make a general scrutiny of their merits and

97

defects, formulate some general rules, and write a book of a few chapters discussing critically the great principles of historical writing.

To Chang, the great principles, not only of historical writing, but of history itself, could be expressed in the word *tao*. Chang avoided defining it directly. I shall imitate him and say only that it has meanings that approximate the following: "internal reality"; "functional balance"; "constitutive equilibrium"; and "spontaneous process of being." The usual, noncommittal translation is "Way."

Chang does not believe that the *tao* of history can be isolated or that it can be defined in abstractions. It is inseparable from its effects. It is (like Aristotle's *form*) the things themselves, but especially the direction in which they move themselves, their internal goal. It is the things in their pushing, pulling, balancing, and shifting. It is the future forming out of the past. It is to nature and everything in it what a man's "self" is to himself. Each man's self is his own, and each self at each moment is not what it was or will be. And yet this elusive something is what one must intuit and be true to.

The ordinary man, says Chang, does what he does without knowing why. But the sage, seeing the ebb and flow of life, acts with insight and creates the laws and institutions that are needed. "One may therefore say that the sage takes part of the *tao*; but one may not say that the sage and the *tao* are substantially the same."

The *tao* lives in human laws and institutions and is the human ability to be civilized at all. But it never remains just what it was, and the response to it that once was useful soon becomes the opposite. A great man sees the failure of his predecessor. He is like the astronomer correcting a preceding theory. But great man and astronomer are never right once for all. Their way of seeing things becomes a fashion, and the fashion becomes excessive. Another great man, or another astronomer, must again make a correction. "When an extreme is reached and it is not counteracted, it will be impossible to attain what is central and corrected." And so ideas and institutions change eternally. Nature is formless, and so there is nothing they can finally be.

This attitude leads Chang to give the historian advice on

his profession. It is useless to expect everyone to be the same. True learning must express one's own nature, and to specialize is only to express that one has a particular, and not a universal nature. Some people are naturally interested in concrete details, others in large wholes. "There is for each man some kind of work for which he is by nature inclined and which he can pursue effectively; thus each man can achieve something of his own. . . . You should not be ashamed because you lack an ability someone else has."

History is a combination of record-keeping, an angular exactness, and intuition, a flexible entrance into meanings and tendencies. Record-keeping looks backward, intuition into the future. Every true historian combines both abilities, but unequally. The ideal balance between them would command both Heaven and Man and glorify the Tao itself.

The Historians' Humanity

As Chinese as they are, the historians we have been discussing are also simply human. They are historians because, like ourselves, they are curious, and because they need the company of the dead and the unborn. We see this openly in Liu Chih-chi. He wants to make people immortal by recording their acts, and himself immortal by becoming part of the record he is making. Scholars, he says, live by communing with the dead and their greatness. History gives us eternity, together with morality:

From emperors and kings down to poor commoners, from courtiers near the throne to distant wayfarers in the mountains and forests, there is none that does not work and strive for merit and fame. Why is this? It is because they think to create an imperishable thing. And what is it that can be called imperishable? It is only to have one's name recorded on bamboo and silk. If formerly the world had been without bamboo and silk, if there had been no historian-officials at the time . . . good and bad would have been indistinguishable, beautiful and ugly would have perished forever. But if historian-officials are not lacking, if bamboo and silk survive, then even though the man himself has perished, vanished into the void, his deeds are as if present, bright as the Milky Way. So scholars who come after can open the wrappers and book-boxes and meet in spirit the men of antiquity, without leaving their own houses they can exhaust a thousand ages. When they see a worthy example they think of emulation, when they see an unworthy one, they examine themselves.

This note rings sharper and more tragically in Ssu-ma Ch'ien. Having defended a general who had lost a campaign, he was punished by castration. As a man of honor, he was supposed to respond to such a disgrace by committing suicide, but he refused to kill himself. Though others might think him a coward, he had been left with the duty of self-expression. Death, he says, is easy, but history is hard. Like other illustrious sufferers and cripples, he will express himself. He would be ashamed, he says, not to be immortal:

If even the lowest slave and scullion maid can bear to commit suicide, why should not one like myself be able to do what has to be done? But the reason I have not refused to bear these ills and have continued to live, dwelling in vileness and disgrace without taking my leave, is that I grieve that I have things in my heart which I have not been able to express fully, and I am ashamed to think that after I am gone my writings will not be known to posterity. Too numerous to record are the men of ancient times who were rich and noble and whose names have yet vanished away. It is only those who were masterful and sure, the truly extraordinary men, who are still remembered. When the Earl of the West was imprisoned at Yu-li, he expanded the *Changes*; Confucius was in distress and he made the *Spring and Autumn*; Ch'ü Yüan was banished and he composed his poem "Encountering Sorrow"; after Tso Ch'iu lost his sight, he composed *Narratives from the States*; when Sun Tzu had had his feet amputated, he set forth the *Art of War*; Lü Pu-wei was banished to Shu, but his *Lü-lan* has been handed down through the ages; while Han Fei Tzu was held prisoner in Ch'in, he wrote "The Difficulties of Disputation" and "The Sorrow of Standing Alone"; most of the three hundred poems of the *Book of Odes* were written when the sages poured forth their anger and dissatisfaction. All these men had a rankling in their hearts, for they were not able to accomplish what they wished. Therefore they wrote about past affairs in order to pass on their thoughts to future generations. Those like Tso Ch'iu, who was blind, or Sun Tzu, who had no feet, could never hold office, so they retired to compose books in order to set forth their thoughts and indignation, handing down their theoretical writings in order to show posterity who they were. I too have ventured not to be modest but have entrusted myself to my useless writings. I have gathered up and brought together the old traditions of the world which were scattered and lost. I have examined the deeds and events of the past and examined the principles behind their success and failure, their rise and decay, in one hundred and thirty chapters. I wished to examine into all that concerns heaven and man, to penetrate the changes of the past and present, completing all as the work of one family. But before I had finished my rough manuscript, I met with this calamity. It is because I regretted that it had not been completed that I submitted to the extreme penalty without rancor. When I have truly completed this work, I shall deposit it in the Famous Mountain. If it may be handed down to men who will appreciate it, and penetrate to the villages and great cities, then though I should suffer a thousand mutilations, what regret should I have? Such matters as these may be discussed with a wise man, but it is difficult to explain them to ordinary people.

The Chinese historians, like others, have a type of cunning, which sometimes becomes conscious. They are engaged in making a curious, uneven mythology, in which they themselves will take part. Mythology seems to exist apart from time, while history seems to be time itself. But history, as formulated by men, affects us like mythology. Both come in place of oblivion or chaos, and both situate us in an area we understand or think we can—emotionally there is no difference. Both, by giving precedents, make us feel that we know what may safely be done. We turn our time into space, with its patterns on the pages of books, we turn what Liu calls our "mayfly-brief life" into something that is sold and bought and read and recalled. That this interests and, as we get older, comforts us, means that Liu and Ssu-ma were essentially right.

4

Cosmographers

TIME, SPACE, WORLD,

GREAT ULTIMATE

HISTORY shows us what we have been, in relation to what we now are. It is a time-map of the general features of human life. Cosmography is the map, not of human life, but of the cosmos, which is the universe seen as an orderly system. Cosmography, the dictionary says, is "a science that describes and maps the main features of the heavens and the earth, including astronomy, geography, and geology." More broadly, it is "a description of the main features of the universe." As cosmographers, most of us are vague. We care less for the cosmos than for the tiny fraction of it we feel at home in. But our thought is influenced by what we suppose the cosmos to be. It lies behind and around us. It is our background, it frames us, as a frame does a picture, as a wall does both frame and picture, as a house a wall, frame, and picture together, as a street a house and everything in it, and so on out to the bounds, if any, of the universe. Consciously or not, we make our final judgments in relation to the universe, to our notion, that is, of how things are finally ordered. Every decision on what *we* are or are not involves one on what the universe we exist in is or is not.

Of all the features of the universe, it is time which feels most intimate. It is our self changing, moving always in the same, first hopeful and then deadly direction. It is our feeling of and toward the past, present, and future, and it therefore is our pride and shame in what we have become, and our hope or fear of what we will come to. But it is also essential to the order by which we live with others. We make long-term plans by the succession of seasons and the time of calendars, and we regulate our days by the succession of light and dark and the time of watches. Time is the flow of our private lives, the current in which we all flow together, and also a basic, impersonal dimension in physics. If we can grasp something of the Chinese idea and experience of time, we will have penetrated somewhat into their mind.

Cosmography releases the imagination. For a moment, then, we can turn speculative—the facts will come soon enough—and think of the time-qualities of Chinese experience. In the order in which we have considered it, this experience relates, first, to their family life, secondly, to their institutional life, thirdly, to their art, and, fourthly, to their conception of history. After we have speculated on time in all these aspects of Chinese life, we will be able to go on to new, cosmographical matters, by which I mean Chinese timekeeping and clocks and calendars, astronomy, and the compass; and Chinese ideas on the evolution of the universe. Finally comes the final background, the Chinese Great Ultimate, which is grasped more by poetic emotion than by abstract thought.

The Time
of Life
and of Art

If we think back to the family lives of the Chinese, we remember the few carefree years of infancy and the shock of an increasingly harsh discipline. We remember that the father was supposed to be distant and severe. The son—we have followed Chinese tradition in ignoring the daughter!— then began a long, tense, exhausting climb up the examination ladder. Even assuming he was successful, his life in the bureaucracy would involve difficulties and long absences from home. To succeed in the bureaucracy meant to live very carefully. And if one lived long enough, one ended by becoming a patriarch. (See Plate XV.)

Considered purely as time, what quality would such a life have? Surely it would be good at both its ends. The first end, of infancy, would mostly be forgotten, but would leave

106

the feeling of someone who could be trusted and some pleasure that could really be had. Maybe the Chinese readiness to assume a utopian beginning to history was made emotionally plausible by the relative utopia that began the life of each individual. It is also possible that the Chinese desire to be spontaneous, confined usually to art but sometimes general and anarchistic, was strengthened by the unconscious attraction of a free infancy. Such an infancy may also help to account for the Taoists' choice of the little child as their ideal. As for the latter end of life, that of the patriarch, it gave dignity to persons even when they had grown weak and were in sight of death. Doted on in infancy, in dotage, revered, a man could keep nostalgia and hope, past and future, in fairly even balance.

Between its two ends, life would have a clear direction. This would in part be given by one's changing family status as one aged and married and acquired children, nephews, nieces, and cousins. There was also, as we cannot forget, the direction provided by the examinations and the successive ranks of the bureaucracy. Although failure was frequent, it usually was possible to try again, and the environmental pressure never disappeared. The scholar-bureaucrats' drive to succeed was therefore strong. Unlike peasants, they had all been educated to aim high. In them, fatalistic resignation must have been the sign, not of lack of ambition, but of its frustration. Briefly, the time of an educated man's life ran along a rising, narrow path with clearly marked heights. Outside this path, there was only resignation, rebellion, or bewilderment.

And what of the time of art? The consciousness of time as regret has already been stressed. The rhythm of language and thought will be discussed in the coming chapter. But the temporal quality of Chinese painting is worth some added comment. Chinese painting, especially when it is close to calligraphy, is filled with motion and so with time. The brushmarks themselves are understood as records of motion; and the relations between brushmarks and between areas, whether full or apparently empty, are motion to the Chinese, a brush-capture of the universal motion. Landscape scrolls invite the motion of eye and mind, often along a literally painted path or river. The painter clears the way for the spectator as if he were really moving through the landscape. The long horizontal scroll, opened a little at a time, is the record of a more complex experience in time, like a motion picture.

There is something, too, in the perspective of a landscape painting that requires motion and time. The atmosphere suggests distance, the mist blocks areas, around which the eye must travel. There is no fixed point for the whole; the angle of view, which is usually from high above, keeps changing. When Li Ch'eng made paintings of buildings that suggested fixed perspective, a critic objected, "If we apply his method to the painting of mountains, we are unable to see more than one layer of the mountain at one time. How then should we see the totality of its unending ranges? . . . Li Ch'eng surely does not understand the principle of viewing the part from the angle of totality. His measurement of height and distance is surely a fine thing. But should one attach paramount importance to the angles and corners of buildings?"

Regardless of what exactly was being objected to, this eleventh-century critic wanted his perspectives shifting and open to motion. Reality is never still, as the Chinese cosmographers will affirm, and a landscape, though only painted, must also be real and never still.

The Single Time of All History

In the early periods of Chinese thought, speculation was especially lively, and not least on time and space. Some philosophers invented paradoxes hard for us to interpret exactly, but that cast doubt on the objectivity of time and space. The Chinese sophists regarded both as relative and said, for instance, that you could go somewhere today and get there yesterday. Later philosophers, joining Taoist and Buddhist ideas, held that space and time were subjective, created by our mind or minds. But the dominant Chinese view is clear: time is real, cyclical, cumulative, and infinite.

Time is real. To the Chinese, society came before all. The family was continuous, beginning with dead ancestors

108

and including the yet unborn. The human obligations that preserved the family and the pride in its continuity made it impossible to devalue time. The recluse or the Buddhist might say otherwise, but if he was not simply playing with ideas, then his opinion was regarded as socially destructive.

Time is cyclical. The Chinese, learning perhaps from the Taoists among them, regarded cosmic processes as similar to those of living things. Forces worked, they believed, in natural cyclical response to one another. One force grew strong, the other weakened, the second grew strong, the first weakened. Cosmic forces worked with the alternation of majestic seesaws. The life-breath breathed in and out; Yin and Yang, female force and male force, moved reciprocally; and the five forces or elements, Wood, Fire, Earth, Metal, and Water, produced one another in cyclical succession. And we have learned that the historians believed history to consist of dynastic cycles.

Time is cumulative and infinite. Although the historians believed in cycles, the cycles were felt to be part of a continuous, cumulative history to which there was no end. Their conception of history might be represented, not by a circle, but by successive loops in a continuous line. Time could not be simply repetitive because it had been marked by unique and dateful events. Their history began with rulers, never to be equaled, of utopian perfection. It was changed forever by the great teacher, Confucius, and differently, though no less, by the emperor who first unified China, in 221 B.C. Not surprisingly, the various calendars that had been used were "harmonized," a single chronology was arrived at, and historians, practicing the art of "meeting and joining," wrote history as a continuous narrative.

Anything else would have been strange. The Chinese awareness of history was too strong, and their records and encyclopedias were too voluminous. Government bureaus, those of astronomy and history among them, piled up documents and summaries of documents, which were studied by the appropriate officials. Collective work was undertaken and recorded in other fields, such as, for example, pharmacology. Reference works recorded every notable invention and discovery, and inventors were deified and honored with temples of their own. In spite of their reverence for the past, therefore, the Chinese did have a sense for the accumulation of knowledge and for technological progress. It was not un-Chinese for an astronomer to propose, toward the beginning of the seventh century A.D., a calendar-correcting survey with the words, "We shall excel the glorious sages of old and resolve our remaining doubts (about the universe). We beg your Majesty not to give credence to the worn-out theories of former times, and not to use them."

Timekeeping, and the Time of Day and Year

No one before us has had such an exact sense of time. The most accurate ancient timepiece, the sundial, could be read to within about a minute of the exact time, but it worked only when the sun was shining. Medieval clocks were accurate to within fifteen minutes a day, early pendulum clocks to within a few seconds, and clocks now in operation to within a thousandth and even a millionth of a second. I doubt if any of the ancient Chinese were as harried by time as we may be. But the Chinese scholar-officials were ambitious men with a full life of study and action, and some of them counted the hours anxiously. Time-anxiety could strike them as it strikes anyone who lives by examinations, conferences, and reports, not to speak of a social conscience. We see this anxiety in an essay, of the first century A.D., on a subject we may think peculiar to ourselves, the saving of time:

The worthies of old, wishing to spread abroad benevolence and righteousness, were always struggling against time. They set no value on whole foot-lengths of jade, but a tenth of an inch of shadow (on the [sun]dial) was as precious as pearls to them. Thus it was that Yü the Great [a semi-legendary culture-hero and hydraulic engineer] raced with time and paid no attention to the enquiries of Nanjung [a character in Chuang Tzu]. Thus it was that Tao Chung never stopped walking till the soles of his feet were as hard as iron. Confucius grudged every moment lost from reading, and Mo Ti was up and about again before his bed had had time to get warm. All these applied their virtue and genius to relieve the miseries of their times, so that they have left a good name behind them through a hundred generations.

Early Chinese sundials show that the day was divided into one hundred equal parts, each of about a quarter of an hour, and this division remained in effect. But the division of the day into twelve hours was the more usual. As everywhere in ancient times, the hours were adjusted to the seasons. That is, the hours assigned to daylight were shortened or lengthened as daylight grew shorter or longer, and the same was done with the hours assigned to night. One of their night-hours or watches could last two and a half hours as we reckon them. Their year, like ours, was divided into twelve months, which they called "moons," and their moons into three periods of ten days or, for "little," twenty-nine-day moons, into two periods of ten days and one of nine.

As will be explained, the establishment and correction of the calendar were of great importance to the Chinese. The reasons were ceremonial, practical, and superstitious, but, in any case, required good records, and so the officials, who were good at record-keeping, recorded solar and lunar eclipses and other heavenly phenomena, including sunspots. We get some feeling for the technical care exerted by the astronomers when we read how the calendar was reformed in 104 B.C.:

They determined the points east and west, set up sundial and gnomons, and contrived water-clocks. With such means they marked out the twenty-eight "Mansions" according to their positions at various points in the four quarters, fixing the first and last days of each month, the equinoxes and solstices, the movements and relative positions of the heavenly bodies, and the phases of the moon.

As a help for making astronomical computations, the Chinese learned to construct celestial globes that rotated automatically. A great globe of this sort was constructed at the capital, on the Emperor's orders, in 1088. The globe was set inside a thirty-foot tower. Above the tower there was a huge armillary sphere (a spherelike set of adjustable rings) for observing the skies. The celestial globe, the armillary sphere, and the figures and gongs that indicated the hours were powered by a water wheel. Most remarkable was the combination of rods, pivoted bars, and levers, technically an escapement, that checked the motions of the wheels and made their speed uniform. This is the first clock escapement we know of, as the whole mechanism is the first astronomical clock drive. (See Plate XVI.)

Time had to be most closely observed, of course, in the cities, and, among city-dwellers, by government officials. At the palace, drums were beaten to signal the beginning of office hours; at lesser government offices, the signal came from a gong or clappers. Officials late to work might be punished with a beating. A thirteenth-century description of Hangchow, then the capital, tells us how the whole city was roused in the morning:

About four or five in the morning, when the bells of the Buddhist and Taoist monasteries have rung, hermit-monks come down from the hills surrounding the town and go about the streets of Hangchow beating their strips of iron or their wooden resonators in the form of a fish, announcing everywhere the dawn. They call out what the weather is like: "It is cloudy," "It is raining," "The sky is clear." In wind, in rain, in snow or in freezing cold, they go out just the same. They also announce any court reception to be held that day, whether a grand or a little or an ordinary audience. In this way the officials in the various government departments, the officers of the watch, and the soldiers whose names are on the list for the watch-towers, are all kept informed and hurry off to their offices or their posts. As for the monk announcers, they go around the town collecting alms on the first and fifteenth of each month as well as on feast-days.

The officials finished their work in the afternoon and spent the rest of the day as they liked. They also received a fixed number of days of leave each year. The death of a parent was followed by an enforced "three-year" leave—in practice, just over two years. During these years, an official's rivals could advance and his enemies intrigue against him, while he could do little more than write, paint, or study.

For the ordinary, nonofficial Chinese, there were few

holidays. Those they did have, they celebrated with the greatest pleasure and talent. The most important for everyone was the New Year. A description of it in thirteenth-century Hangchow may convey why it was so loved by the Chinese.

Preparations began a whole month in advance. Snow was a sign of good luck—and you could make doglike lions of it. Toward the end of the month, shopkeepers would give away quantities of lucky paper streamers to their customers. The ancestors of the family and the guardian spirits of the house were given offerings and asked to make the coming year peaceful and healthy. A noisy procession chased pestilences out through the Gate of the Eastern Flowering.

New Year's day itself and the two following days were quiet. They were spent celebrating at home with the family. People went out mainly to wish their friends a Happy New Year. Much the most impressive ceremony took place at the palace:

At dawn on New Year's day, as soon as the bells at the palace had stopped ringing, the Emperor burnt incense and addressed prayers to Heaven asking for a good harvest in the coming year, while the court officials, dressed in ceremonial robes, stood at the door of the temple where the sovereign was officiating. Delegates from every prefecture in the empire and foreign ambassadors came to offer him gifts.

On a date that was fixed according to the solar calendar, and which corresponded to February 5th—the day of the "establishment of spring"—an official festival was celebrated by officials of the court and of the prefectures. It was an agrarian festival. The evening before, a procession of singing-girls and of men beating drums went to the prefectural building in search of the "spring ox." This was a small clay animal that had to be taken to the imperial palace at dawn the next day by the prefect and the prefectural officials and employees. On that day, ministers and court officials received from the Emperor head-ornaments and little streamers made of gold and silver thread which they hung on their heads. Presents of the same kind, tokens of good wishes for the New Year, were exchanged between private individuals.

The real outburst of celebration, the Feast of Lanterns, took place on the 14th, 15th, and 16th of the first moon. For three days and nights, people overate, overdrank, and overspent. Lanterns and streamers hung everywhere, and if you looked at the city from afar, it was all like a bonfire. A bonfire outside, a carnival inside, with musicians, acrobats, costumed dancers, and marionette shows, pipes, drums, and the moving stars of lanterns. Pretty girls and noisy young men, of course, and drunkenness, and a big show at the palace. Till it was time to be sober and poor again.

Astrological Astronomers and Astronomical Jesuits

In the matter of astronomy, tradition, which has been hinted at above, was old and urgent. The Chinese, a nation of ceremony-bound farmers, were fixed in their yearly actions by the calendar circulated in the Emperor's name. Because the relation between the agricultural seasons and official calendar dates kept changing, the farmers had to be told what it would be. But the Emperor did more than furnish agricultural information. He kept the world stable. His astronomers or astrologers noted the portents, the shooting stars, meteors, comets, eclipses, and conjunctions, and issued warnings and recommendations. The Emperor might have to take ceremonial action against some threatening evil. Then, as on the occasion of the New Year, he might ascend to the great altar, address himself to Heaven, which was the Emperor-on-High, to the August Earth, to his Imperial Ancestors, mythical and real, to the Planets, and to the Stars, and try to hold the balance of the universe steady and beneficent.

The Chinese had made remarkable observations and had constructed remarkable astronomical instruments. They had inherited some Moslem astronomy as well. How it happened that they lost so much, as it appears, of their technical proficiency, I do not know. Perhaps it had been concentrated in the hands of too few men. When Jesuit missionaries got to Peking, in the early seventeenth century, they decided that a European astronomer or mathematician —the two were hardly distinguished—could gain them influence and converts. Seven thousand books were gathered in Europe, together with clocks, telescopes, and other astronomical instruments. Galileo was solicited for advice, which he understandably refused, but Kepler was glad to send information.

The state of Chinese astronomy is described in a report made by a Jesuit then at Peking. The report, dated September 1, 1612, says, among other things:

For the Chinese there exist two branches of mathematics of which the first is called *t'ien-wên* and the second *li-fa*. *T'ien-wên*, strictly speaking, is what we call fortunetelling. *Li-fa* has to do with the calendar and the movements of the celestial bodies theoretically and practically.

T'ien-wên or fortunetelling is prohibited by Chinese law so that save for the mathematicians of the Royal College to whom it appertains officially nobody can study it. *Li-fa* or astronomy, in our sense of the word, is not prohibited and may be studied by anybody. . . . But since mathematics is commonly called *t'ien-wên* among the Chinese, the general idea is that it is prohibited and that nobody may study it. But even so, the fact remains that the kings founded a bureau or special college for this science, and that its members have no other duty than to calculate eclipses, to make the calendar each year, and to observe the stars, the comets, and other prodigious phenomena of the sky, daily and nightly, for the purpose of advising the king and of declaring whether these are good or evil omens. For others besides the official members of this bureau or college to do this work is prohibited under grave sanctions—I mean for them to do the work publicly so that all may know, because privately many who are not members actually do the work.

There are only two colleges of these mathematicians in all China: one in this city of Peking, the other in Nanking. The members are honored mandarins who live on the treasury and whose positions are inherited by their sons. The sons, however, are admitted to succession only after examination.

The rules followed by this college for the computation of eclipses and compilation of the calendar had already been corrected 55 times, according to the *Histories*, that is if we are to assume that the same rules were used in antiquity. The last correction was made 300 years ago, during the lifetime of a famous mathematician named Kuo Shou-ching. . . .

The Chinese lack works on mathematics, whether treating of planetary theory or of other scientific or speculative subjects in our European sense. They lack such treatises whether of native or of Mohammedan origin. Hence, even the members of the royal college of mathematicians do not know how to do anything except predict eclipses, tell fortunes, and point out propitious and unpropitious places for building, burying, and the like.

Therefore, when they saw so many of our books treating of things in a scientific manner, such as the first six *Books of Euclid*, translated by Dr. Paul and Father Matthew Ricci, of happy memory, they wanted them for themselves, because they are talented and love science. . . .

Since the Chinese have no planetary theory but only the tables of which we have spoken, they cannot scientifically correct the errors in the movements of the planets in which consists the correction of their calendar. . . . If the Chinese attach so much importance to this correction and if the greatest of the court are occupied with it, it is because in their calendar they indicate the things which one ought to do on such and such a day and at such and such an hour, especially in regard to the dead, a very important matter in China. They say that if there is an error in the day and hour of the winter solstice, all the days of the year will be wrong, because one says that it is such and such a day when it is not; and if the conjunction of the moon is mistaken, equally also the days and hours are mistaken. In such a case the whole kingdom is deceived by its great prejudice because people do not do the things on the day and at the hour when they would find the luck which they ought to have.

The Jesuit astronomers were diligent. One of them dictated a short treatise on the telescope to a Christian Chinese, who translated it. It recommended the telescope as an instrument capable of abolishing distance and allowing one to see the attacks of brigands or pirates ahead of time. A later treatise stressed the military importance of the telescope. The Emperor grew interested, and in 1634, a Christian convert, who had become director of the Astronomical Bureau, presented him with "a telescope, two copperguards for the telescope, a cloth of silk brocade, a box of the finest yellow silk for the telescope, a wooden stand."

116

By then, a contest between the rival astronomical groups, Europeans, Chinese, and Chinese using Mohammedan tables, had already taken place, and the official astronomers, who had predicted an eclipse less accurately than the Jesuits, had been fined three months' salary. In 1629, the three groups made rival estimates of the time of an eclipse. The Jesuits won and were entrusted with the reform of the calendar. They won still another contest about thirty years later. Their leader, Adam Schall, saved the "Mohammedan" loser from the death his disgrace had earned him.

Real hatred had now been aroused. The displaced head of the Bureau of Astronomy, allied with the Mohammedan astronomers, the Buddhist monks, and the Court eunuchs, laid three accusations against the Jesuits: high treason, preaching of a false religion, and spreading of false astronomical knowledge. The second charge was accepted, the third put to the test. Chinese, Mohammedan, and Christian estimates were made of an eclipse that was due. The Christians won, as they had before; but their victory was not enough, and they and their astronomy were condemned.

The ironic parallel with Galileo's trial need not be stressed. But whereas Galileo was sentenced to house arrest and partial silence, Schall and his Chinese aides were sentenced to be beheaded, and when this punishment came to seem too mild, to be sliced up alive.

European science condemned the Jesuits in Chinese eyes. Chinese superstition now saved them. A terrific earthquake shook the capital and killed 300,000 people. A dust storm filled the air. Fire broke out in the palace itself. These omens were so powerful that the Jesuits were released. Adam Schall did not survive for long. His companion and successor was later appointed head of the Bureau of Astronomy. Here we end our story of the Jesuit intervention in the cosmography of the Chinese.

The Compass

Astronomy has its own instruments that provoke thought and make exactness possible. But every device that measures can serve as a cosmographical tool. The use of such a device adds precision to thought as much as to the hand. Indirectly, then, the language in which the Chinese praise their measuring instruments is cosmographical talk. The following is an example.

The plumb-line serves to align the ten-thousand things, the water-level to level them, the compasses to round them, the steelyard to equalize them, the square to square them and the balance to weigh them. The plumb-line as a measure is erect and unswerving. . . . From antiquity until today its straightness has remained unchangeable. Vast and profound is its virtue, broad and great so that it can encompass all things. This is why the Rulers of Old used it as the prime standard of all things.

Of the cosmographical tools, as I shall call them, invented by the Chinese, the compass was outstanding. It began, perhaps, as a lodestone used for a divination game that may have resembled chess. Its earliest clear description goes back to about the year 1090. "Magicians," it says, "rub the point of a needle with the lodestone; then it is able to point to the south. But it always inclines slightly to the east, and does not point directly at the south. It may be made to float on the surface of the water, but it is then rather unsteady. . . . It is best to suspend it by a single cocoon fiber of new silk attached to the center of the needle by a piece of wax the size of a mustard-seed—then, hanging in a windless place, it will always point to the south."

A text only slightly later describes the use of the compass for navigating ships:

According to the government regulations concerning sea-going ships, the larger ones can carry several hundred men, and the smaller ones may have more than a hundred men on board. . . . The ship's pilots are acquainted with the configuration of the coasts; at night they steer by the stars, and in the daytime by the sun. In dark weather they look at the south-pointing needle. They also use a line a hundred feet long with a hook at the end, which they let down to take samples of mud from the sea-bottom; by its appearance and smell they can determine their whereabouts.

118

Cosmic Questions,
Answering Forces

The question where we are can be answered with a chart, a compass, and sea-bottom mud. But if the question is asked, not in relation to sea and shore, but to everything, the "Where are we?" becomes the same as "What are we?" This joint question is in every sense the universal one; but each tradition learns to put it in a different spirit, and to phrase it so as to suggest the kind of answers it prefers. We can see this for China if we listen to the cosmic questions put by an early Chinese philosopher:

Does heaven turn? Does the earth sit still? Do sun and moon compete for a place to shine? Who masterminds all this? Who pulls the strings? Who, resting inactive himself, gives the push that makes it go this way? I wonder, is there some mechanism that works it and won't let it stop? I wonder if it just rolls and turns and can't bring itself to a halt? Do the clouds make the rain, or does the rain make the clouds? Who puffs them up, who showers them down like this? Who, resting inactive himself, stirs up all this lascivious joy? The winds rise in the north, blowing now west, now east, whirling up to wander on high. Whose breaths and exhalations are they? Who, resting inactive himself, huffs and puffs them about like this?

These questions suggest Chinese answers. They suggest that beings or forces occur in correlative, answering pairs—heaven and earth, sun and moon, inaction and pushing, breaths and exhalations, and huffing and puffing. They suggest that the ultimate source is inactive, that the activity of nature may be consciously guided or automatic, and that its activity is sexual.

The Chinese never gave the questions a uniform answer. But in the course of time they developed and joined a number of old ideas, those of an ultimate beginning, of a cosmic breath, of a male and a female force, and of a set of five cosmic elements. To most later Chinese thinkers, the relationship between beginning, breath, sexual forces, and agents explained the universe. It was both their physics and their metaphysics.

The idea of the breath, the *ch'i*, that animates nature is all-important, we remember, to the Chinese theory of art. *Ch'i* is breath, air, ether, gas, force. It has been conceived of, under other names, in other traditions, and it originates in the analogy between the wind and our own breathing. The wind penetrates everywhere. It has a wayward, energetic, sometimes violent nature that makes it alive; and to the farmer it brings and disperses life in the form of rain. Because our own life depends on breathing, it is easy to suppose that we live and exert force because we contain or are the wind that is life and force. But can the world be *ch'i* alone? Yes, if like water it can change from a fluid to a gaseous or solid state, all different manifestations of the same force or substance. And where does the *ch'i* come from? Before anything existed, it was, maybe, Emptiness, an infinitely thin, uncharacterizable simplicity, and then, maybe, there came the Great Beginning. This may not seem a satisfying answer, but it inhibits further questioning. (See Plate XVII.)

The origin of male and female forces is as obvious as that of cosmic breath. Beginning in our own life, the idea is extended to complementary forces everywhere. The traditional Chinese judges females and female force negatively. I assume that a female philosopher, had one existed in China, would have protested. But the female, though negative, cannot be dispensed with—remember, "Girls too are necessary!"

By analogy, then, the female force or Yin is passive and weak. By further analogy, it is destructive, that is, it makes things (including men) passive and weak. It is internality, darkness, cloudiness, rain, autumn, and winter. The male force or Yang is positive, active, strong, and constructive. It is light, heat, spring, and summer.

What relation is there between Yin and Yang and cosmic breath? The solution is simply that the two forces are different forms of the one. As Chu Hsi wrote, "Although Yin and Yang are two different words, it is actually but the shrinking and growing of one fluid, an advancing and retreating, a shrinking and expanding. The advancing is Yang, the retreating Yin; the growing Yang and the shrinking Yin. It is only a process taking place between heaven and earth incessantly from times immemorial through the shrinking and expanding of this one fluid. Therefore one may say, Yin and Yang are one, but one may also say that they are two things."

There does not seem to have been any original connection between the Yin-Yang experts, as they were called, and the exponents of the Five Elements. But both theories came to be classed together as belonging to the Yin-Yang School. Like the other ideas we have been discussing, that of the Five Elements or, better, Agents or "Movers," also has an obvious psychological origin. It is a collection of the substances that look to the primitive eye as if they were the stuff of everything else. They are regarded, in Greece and India too, as forces. They belong, that is, to the primitive-sophisticated thinking that does not distinguish between force and substance.

The Five Agents are Wood, Fire, Earth, Metal, and Water. The philosophers found it difficult to correlate them with the seasons, which had always been reckoned as four. Earth was therefore assigned to the center and regarded as distributed over the whole year, or as ruling from the center like a modest emperor who himself occupied no special territory.

At first only the most natural correlations were made. It is easy to see why wood was correlated with the spring, the color green, and the east; fire with summer, red, and south; earth with center and yellow; metal with autumn, white, and west; and water with winter, black, and north. But the correlations multiplied quickly, to a number and complexity that seem good only for compulsive pedants or omnivorous ritualists. A basic, relatively early list attaches each Agent to its own season, day, emperor, guardian spirit, type of animal, musical note, number, taste, smell, sacrifice, bodily organ, and color.

The Agents were conceived to be both simultaneous and successive—they were simultaneously present, but ruled in succession. In keeping with this notion, each historical dynasty adopted an Agent and its color for flags, ceremonial clothing, and ritual. The following dynasty was then supposed to adopt the succeeding Agent and color. The Agents could also be correlated with the structure and function of government, as they are in the following slightly paranoidal way:

Wood is the agent of the Minister of Agriculture. . . . Now wood is the agent of agriculture, and agriculture is the occupation of the people. If the people are not compliant but revolt, then the Minister of the Interior is ordered to punish the leaders of the rebellion and set things right. Therefore we say metal overcomes wood. . . . Metal is the agent of the Minister of the Interior. If he is weak and does not know how to use the officers and men properly, the Minister of War must punish him. Therefore we say fire overcomes metal. . . . It is water that administers the law, therefore we say that water overcomes fire. Water is the agent of the Minister of Justice. . . . If the administrator is prejudiced and unfair, using the law only to punish people, then the Minister of Works must execute him. Therefore we say that earth overcomes water. . . . If the king is extravagant and wasteful, exceeding all bounds and forgetting propriety, then the people will rebel and when the people rebel, the ruler is lost. Therefore we say wood overcomes earth.

I have been quoting from Tung Chung-shu (179?–104? B.C.). A stern, orderly man, he helped lay the basis for Confucian orthodoxy and for the examination system. He combined the social teachings of Confucius with the metaphysical cosmography of the Yin-Yang School. Although I have called his correlation slightly paranoidal, it must be remembered that his aim was to impress on people that they and the universe should make up one harmonious system. The wind of love is mild, he said, and the wind of wrath is chill. Like Heaven, the ruler should be seasonable, applying mildness and wrath for the sake of prosperity. "Heaven, earth, and man are one, and therefore the passions of man are one with the seasons of Heaven. So the time and place for each must be considered. If Heaven produced heat in the time for cold, or cold in the season of heat, then the year must be bad, while if the ruler manifests anger when joy would be appropriate, or joy when anger is needed, then the age must fall into chaos."

Tung Chung-shu put the cosmic forces into a relationship that remained typically Chinese. It was only the sage, he said, who could relate the many to the one and so link them to the Origin, which permeates Heaven and Earth and is the root of all things. The unity of things was also their common possession of *ch'i*:

Collected together, the ethers (*ch'i*) of the universe constitute a unity; divided, they constitute the Yin and Yang; quartered they constitute the four seasons; still further sundered, they constitute the Five Elements. These elements represent movement. Their movements are not identical. Therefore they are referred to as the Five Movers. These Five Movers constitute five officiating powers. Each in turn gives birth to the next and is overcome by the next but one in turn.

Of the Yin and Yang in particular, Tung says:

Within the universe exist the ethers (*ch'i*) of the Yin and Yang. Men are constantly immersed in them, just as fish are constantly immersed in water. The difference between them and water is that the turbulence of the latter is visible, whereas that of the former is invisible. . . . In the universe there seems to be a nothingness and yet there is substance. Men are constantly immersed in this eddying mass, with which, whether themselves orderly or disorderly, they are carried along in a common current.

Of the Five Elements, Tung says:

Wood is the starting point of the cycle of the Five elements, water is its conclusion, and earth its center. Such is their heavenly sequence. Wood produces fire, fire earth, earth metal, metal water, and water wood. Such is their father-and-son relationship. . . . Each of them exercises its own capacities in the performance of its official duties.

Cosmography
as Ethics

I should like to sum up the cosmographic development we have been following. I shall do so by means of a quotation from the philosopher, Chou Tun-i (1017–1073). He is generally looked on as the founder of Neo-Confucianism, which dominated the later thought of China. Chu Hsi said of him that he had succeeded only in outlining the truth, but that it was the whole truth he had outlined. When this truth came to prevail, said Chu Hsi, scholars were no longer attracted by the writing of vulgar essays or seduced by Buddhist heresies.

Chou Tun-i was esthetic, metaphysical, and ethical: he achieved the esthetic integration of Yin-Yang metaphysics with Confucian ethics. The product was, approximately, official Chinese thought, a rather tight, bureaucratically neat universe, but one that most Chinese lived in most of the time. He had arrived at a sufficient ethical cosmography or cosmographic ethics. I quote enough—over half—of his *Explanation of the Diagram of the Great Ultimate* to make this clear:

The Non-ultimate and also the Great Ultimate! The Great Ultimate through movement generates Yang. When its activity reaches its limit, it becomes tranquil. Through tranquillity the Great Ultimate generates Yin. When tranquillity reaches its limit, activity begins again. So movement and tranquillity alternate and become the root of each other, giving rise to the distinction of Yin and Yang, and the two modes are thus established.

By the transformation of Yang and its union with Yin, the Five Agents of Water, Fire, Wood, Metal, and Earth arise. When these five material forces (*ch'i*) are distributed in harmonious order, the four seasons run their course.

The Five Agents constitute one system of Yin and Yang, and Yin and Yang constitute one Great Ultimate. The Great Ultimate is fundamentally the Non-ultimate. The Five Agents arise, each with its specific nature.

When the reality of the Non-ultimate and the essence of Yin, Yang, and the Five Agents come into mysterious union, integration ensues. Heaven constitutes the male element, and Earth constitutes the female element. The interaction of these two material forces engenders and transforms the myriad things. The myriad things produce and reproduce, resulting in an unending transformation.

It is man alone who receives the material forces in their highest excellence, and therefore he is most intelligent. This physical form appears, and his spirit develops consciousness. The five moral principles of his nature (humanity, righteousness, propriety, wisdom, and faithfulness) are aroused by, and react to, the external world and engage in activity; good and evil are distinguished; and human affairs take place.

124

The Universe
a Globe

The cosmographic map is still incomplete. We have not yet given the universe its shape. According to one theory, it had none. The sun, moon, and stars just float freely in empty space, their movements and rest caused by air. According to a second theory, the universe was hemispherical. "Heaven," it said, "is like an umbrella, earth like an overturned dish. Both heaven and earth are high in the middle and slope down at the edges. . . . The sun, moon, and stars alternately shine and are hidden and this makes the day and night." According to a third theory, the universe was spherical, with heaven wrapping the earth as a shell wraps the yolk of an egg.

It was this last theory, of the "encircling heaven," that was adopted by most later thinkers, Chu Hsi among them. Chu Hsi supposed that in the beginning, Yin and Yang circulated and moved, gathered speed, and pushed sediment toward the center of the universe, where it solidified as the earth. The universe so formed is held together by the speed of its rotation. The earth is still. The air closest to it is turbid and slow-turning, but the successive strata of air, nine in number, are successively more pure and quick. The purer and quicker they are, the more compressed and hard they become. The outermost stratum is the purest, quickest, and hardest, and it forms a shell around the universe. If heaven stopped rotating for even a minute, the waters that surround the earth would spill out and the earth would tumble down.

Cosmic Evolution and
Cosmic Rationality

Chu Hsi claimed that men and all living things would perish in chaos and then begin anew; but he believed, as we have seen, that the universe had been formed by a process of evolution, and it was, he said, indestructible. He believed that we could still come on evidence of its formation. "If today," he said, "we climb the high mountains and look around, we will see ranges of mountains in the shapes of waves. This is because the water formed them like this, though we do not know in what period they solidified." He also drew attention to the conches and oyster shells, sometimes embedded in stones, which are seen on high mountains. The mountains, he said, must once have been under water.

There is nothing in Chinese thought antagonistic to the idea of evolution, and Buddhism encouraged it, though in the sense of repeating cycles. We therefore find hints and statements of biological and social evolution. History could give the Chinese a solid idea of social evolution. But for biological evolution, I have seen only haphazardly reasoned texts, of which the earliest, most curious, and most haphazard comes from Chuang Tzu:

> The seeds of things have mysterious workings. In the water they become Break Vine, on the edges of the water they become Frog's Robe. If they sprout on the slopes they become Hill Slippers. If Hill Slippers get rich soil, they turn into Crow's Feet. The roots of Crow's Feet turn into maggots and their leaves turn into butterflies. Before long the butterflies are transformed and turn into insects that live under the stove. . . . Sheep's Groom couples with bamboo that has not sprouted for a long while and produces Green Peace plants. Green Peace plants produce leopards and leopards produce horses and horses produce men. Men in time return again to the mysterious workings. So all creatures come out of the mysterious workings and go back into them again.

Among the Chinese, as among ourselves, there was argument over the rationality of the universe. Philosophical Taoists might easily think of it as spontaneous, without any directing consciousness. Philosophers who held this position included Wang Ch'ung (27–100?) and Wang Fu-chih (1619–1692). "When Heaven moves," said Wang Ch'ung, "it does not desire to produce things thereby, but things are produced of their own accord: such is spontaneity. When it gives forth its ether, it does not desire to create things, but things are created of themselves: such is non-activity. . . . Cold and warmth are dependent on Heaven and Earth and are linked with the Yin and Yang. How can human affairs or the administration of the country have any influence on them?" Wang Fu-chih, who considered himself a loyal Neo-Confucian, saw that many things in the world supported one another's existence. But this was only, he explained, by the power of impersonal force and by the mutual relationships of environment and living things, the science of which *we* call "ecology."

But these views were not typical, and could not be in the moral climate of China. The most usual opinion among later Chinese thinkers can again be represented by Chu Hsi. He was perfectly sure that there was no manlike being in heaven who judges evildoers. But his universe was not morally neutral. Like the Stoics, he believed that it was impersonally rational and, as rational, wholly good. He concentrated this belief in his idea of the Great Ultimate:

The Great Ultimate is simply the principle of the highest good. Each and every person has in him the Great Ultimate and each and every thing has in it the Great Ultimate. What Master Chou [Chou Tun-i] calls the Great Ultimate is a name to express all the virtues and the highest good in Heaven and Earth, man, and things.

I have compared Chu Hsi with the Stoics. His words will also bring Plato and Aristotle to mind. I will not attempt the comparison here, but end instead with his human and cosmic rule, "Those who do violence to their nature destroy themselves."

5

Philosophers

FORMS OF LANGUAGE

AND THOUGHT

THE Chinese language is a unique and impressive creation. In its literary forms, with which we are here concerned, it is a particularly artificial creation. Those twentieth-century intellectuals who revolted against it considered it to be as absurdly crippling as the traditional bindings on women's feet. It never served the most natural purposes of language, for no one spoke it. It was something written by a brush and perceived by a mind. Read aloud, in whatever dialect, it would nearly always be too ambiguous to be understood. Only a small minority of the Chinese could use it with freedom, which they had won by intensive study. The others respected it because it was an accomplishment that conferred power on its users. It was, in fact, one of the symbols of power. Its merest scraps were supposed to be handled with respect. It is hard to imagine how, without it, China could have been governed, or how so many able men of so many different kinds could have participated in its culture.

It is therefore easy to think of the language as itself shaping the culture that it expressed, and, in that sense, as China's greatest heritage. In the words of a contemporary Chinese scholar, "It is the Chinese language that has, among other things, shaped Chinese thoughts and philosophy, determined the nature and styles of Chinese literature and arts, accounted at least in part for the failure of traditional China to develop science, and contributed to the moulding of a civilization that is uniquely Chinese."

What exactly is the uniqueness of the language, and what are its mutual relations with the rest of Chinese culture? A specialist in Chinese philosophy, A. C. Graham, believes that the language is centered in human needs and, just because of this, resists ordinary formal logic. It is, he says,

too complex to be laid out in all its interrelations even when it concerns the most trivial everyday matters; when we try to convince someone else we can only pick out key phrases in our thought in order to guide him in the same directions, and try to fill the gaps when he refuses to make the same leaps, but without hope of achieving full logical rigor. The Chinese, like Europeans who are exclusively interested in action or in contemplative experience, have tended to distrust too logical thinkers who insist on filling all the gaps, seeing them as triflers with unimportant questions and gross simplifiers of important ones. . . . The Chinese have been much more impressed by the opposite extreme of intelligence, the aphoristic genius who guides thought of the maximum complexity with the minimum of words, of which the *Tao te ching* presents one of the world's supreme examples.

Having said this, obviously in praise, Graham tries to express just what it is in Chinese that makes it appear to us so careless of logic and that allows it, all the same, to be or to look so clear:

It seems likely, although no one yet has even clearly identified the elusive problems involved, that this general indifference to logical problems is somehow connected with the structure of the Chinese language. In Indo-European languages word-inflection forces us to think in categories, such as thing, quality, and action, past, present, and future, singular and plural, the muddles and inconsistencies of which show us that the forms of thought present difficulties as well as its content; but in Chinese words are uninflected and their functions marked only by particles and by word-order, so that there is a much more complete illusion of looking through language at reality as though through a perfectly transparent medium.

This is provocative. But before we can take up such comparisons, something must be said about the nature of literary Chinese. I begin at the beginning, with the Chinese characters.

The Chinese
Characters

Chinese characters originated, it is assumed, as pictures or diagrams, like those we still recognize in Egyptian hieroglyphics. On this assumption, written Chinese was originally nothing more than a series of simplified pictures of objects, that is, pictographs, and of symbols of ideas, that is, ideographs. "Tree" was the picture of a tree, "sun" of a sun, and "man" of a man. As examples of ideographs, we may take the short horizontal line that means "one," the two such parallel lines that mean "two," the character with a line pointing down and meaning "down," and the similar, opposite one meaning "up."

Further meanings are created by combining or assembling characters. Two trees is "forest." A sun above a tree is "high" or "bright." A sun and moon together are also "bright." A woman and a child together mean "love." A sun with a short horizontal line below it is "dawn." In compounds, a horizontal line, the "one," hints at the meaning, when below, of "foundation," "base," "support," or the like.

Obviously, the characters so far described mean whatever they do regardless of how they are pronounced. They no more depend on pronunciation than the pointing hand we use on signs to mean "in that direction," or than numerals, which have the same meaning in English, French, and German, or even than the red and green traffic lights that mean, respectively, "stop" and "go." But characters can also be used phonetically, to stand for another word having the same sound—as if we wrote "son" with a picture of the sun.

Because the phonetic use of characters is confusing, most characters have both a phonetic component and a "radical" (also called a "determinative" or "signific"). The radical is a sign that shows the general meaning of the character, its category. For example, one component of the character for "sugar" is a phonetic which, when alone, is simply a name. The other component is the radical, "rice," which signifies that the character belongs to a class of foodstuffs.

Chinese characters are and are not words in our sense. If we define "words" as the smallest units of language with a more or less independent meaning, then the Chinese characters fit the definition about as well as the letter combinations we call "words." Like our words, Chinese characters often change in meaning as their context changes. Even in the same general context, a word may have many meanings. A Westerner learning Chinese undergoes the difficulty that a Chinese learning English would have in understanding a text such as: "The head officer had a real head on his shoulders. Marching headily at the head of his troops, he headed them toward the head of the ridge. 'Heads up!' he called to them. 'If we fail, I'll have your heads!' "

This text I have artificially concocted suggests what in Western eyes is the major peculiarity of Chinese. Its characters are more like word roots than words, because they never change. They are never inflected and never add prefixes or suffixes. They have no tense, number, gender, person, or case. The same character serves for "man," "men," and "manhood." To speak of the first person only, the same character serves for "I had gone," "I went," "I have been going," "I am going," "I go," "I will go," and "I will have gone." Although there is a distinction in Chinese that corresponds somewhat to that between verb and noun, it is nevertheless true that the language has no grammar in our usual sense of the word. It must, of course, have a grammar in the sense of the principles that make it intelligible; but these are apparently so complex that they are difficult to learn abstractly, and effectively mastered only by the traditional method of prolonged and attentive use. If we reflect that the rules of English grammar are not in themselves enough to teach us good English, we may not be so puzzled by the absence of explicit grammar in Chinese.

In relation to the Western languages, Chinese has something of the advantage of a picture over a word constructed of letters. As I have said, this advantage was of incalculable importance in unifying China. Writing could be made uniform much more easily than speech. Furthermore, literary Chinese is very terse, and very good, therefore, for the economical recording of everything that has to go into official archives. Some critics think that its terseness makes Chinese a superior language for poetry as well. It allows the maximum of content to be compressed into the minimum of space. Chinese poetry is dense.

The greatest difficulty of Chinese is its ambiguity. This is not the necessary result of the omission of tense, number, gender, and so on. When I say, in English, "Reading is pleasant," I do not necessarily have to specify where, when, how, and to whom it is pleasant. The idea may be disputed, but it is clear enough. The qualifications we have to make in English can be made in Chinese if the writer thinks it necessary. But if they are not necessary, why put them in?

Because terseness was a natural, useful, and pleasing quality of written Chinese, writers accentuated it. They gloried in pun-streaked, allusive brevity. Telegrammatic in style and retentive in memory, they needed cryptographers and mnemonists to read them. But maybe I am exaggerating.

To Be or
Not to Be

"To be" is a very conspicuous verb in English and the other Indo-European languages. Classical Chinese does not have such a verb, either as a copula, joining subject and predicate (the "is" of "The horse is white"), or even perhaps as the expression of existence. It may be impossible to make an adequate translation into Chinese of Descartes' famous declaration, "I think, therefore I am."

The problem of existence is so central to Western philosophy that the absence of the verb "to be" in Chinese might indicate a basic philosophical difference. Indian and European philosophy have never freed themselves from the related problem of substance and attribute, which arises partly because the copula "to be" looks identical with "to be" meaning "to exist." We say, for example, "The horse is white," and tend to think of the horse as something that has, acquires, or loses the attribute of whiteness. In both Indian and European philosophy, existence itself may be thought of as a separable quality that can be added to a possible form. Perhaps because of his language, the Chinese philosopher found it relatively hard to arrive at a sharp substance-attribute distinction. The Buddhists, on the other hand, who normally denied the distinction, imported it into China by way of their polemics.

Judgments

The uniqueness of the Chinese language is easy to see. It is less easy to see if this uniqueness carries over into Chinese thought and, if it does, to what effect. Can Chinese be considered inferior or superior as a language, and, as inferior, superior, or simply different, is it so from a logical, esthetic, or existential point of view? It is hard to answer such questions without cultural prejudice, and impossible, I think, without philosophical bias. Westerners have often been condescending, and Chinese, either proud or zealous for reform.

To give an idea of the many opinions that have been expressed, I shall summarize those of six scholars, each of whom has, in his own way, earned the right to a hearing.

This first opinion is that of John Fryer. From 1868 to 1896 he served the Chinese government as translator of scientific and technological books, which ranged from naval gunnery to shipbuilding, navigation, coal mining, lithography, biology, chemistry, mathematics, and medicine. His work could not have been easy. "Nothing but a strong sense of duty," he wrote, "and a belief that this kind of labour is one of the most effective means under Divine guidance for bringing about the intellectual and moral regeneration of this great country has suffered to render endurable to the translator the long and weary years of close and continuous application which it has involved."

Fryer, whose opinion is obviously worth having, found that even his kind of translation, involving whole new attitudes and terminologies, was possible because, as he said, the Chinese language, like other languages, was capable of growth. Having learned to value Chinese and to condemn those who did not, he wrote, in 1891:

136

We must carefully avoid standing in our own light if we want the Chinese to respect our Western learning. Our systems have no more right to universal use than the Chinese. Their ancient and wonderful language which for some reasons is more suited to become the universal language of the world than any other, must not be tampered or trifled with by those who wish to introduce our Western sciences.

From the opinion of Fryer, we move to that of Alfred Forke, a learned, pioneering historian of Chinese philosophy. In 1927, he emphasized the rhetoric, the ambiguity, the peculiar categories, and the impersonality of Chinese thought. It is possible, he said, to express oneself quite clearly in Chinese, but the Chinese are much more interested in good style than in clarity. They have developed a dense, rhetorical style, in which sentences are constructed in a repetitive, that is, parallel or antithetical way, in either case often at the cost of the logic. Instead of deducing soberly from abstract concepts, they prefer striking images, which can be interpreted differently. The earlier philosophical texts are therefore hard, even for a Chinese, and sometimes near-impossible to understand without a commentary.

Although the origins of the Chinese characters may be forgotten, Forke continues, the Chinese relate them to concrete things, and so tend to think concretely rather than abstractly. Another kind of problem is caused by the use of radicals. These establish the categories of thought. For example, the words that express thinking or feeling are put under the radical "heart." For this reason, the Chinese, including their philosophers, have assumed that all the spiritual functions are located in the heart.

As for logic, says Forke, in the early period of Chinese philosophy, the active debating that was carried on led to the exploration of this discipline. Even in this early period, however, logical thought was obstructed by the absence in Chinese of such categories as subject, predicate, and object. The absence was related to the general impersonality or collectivism of the Chinese.

The third opinion is that of Chang Tung-sun, known in China as a specialist in Western thought. A translator of Plato and Bergson, he was a partisan of Kant, before, that is, he became a Marxist. The essay that I am about to cite first appeared in 1938.

Every form of logic, says Chang, is related to a given form of culture and language. Western logicians assume that theirs is the universal logic of human reason. But it is based on the structure of the Western languages, and therefore not universal. Chinese logic, the logic inherent in the Chinese language, is not, like the Western, based on the subject-predicate relationship or on the so-called "law of identity." It is what might be called "correlation-logic," or "the logic of correlative duality." Its structure is that of relationships, between, for example, something and nothing, or above and below. It uses antonyms to make an idea complete. By the logic of Chinese, one says, "A great sound but scarcely audible," or "Nonresistance means strength." "To sell" is defined by "to buy," because both are the same transaction viewed from opposite standpoints:

From this it is seen that Chinese thought is not based upon the law of identity, but takes as its starting point relative orientation or rather the relation of opposites. This type of thought evidently constitutes a different system. This system is probably related to the nature of Chinese characters. Being ideographic, Chinese characters put emphasis on the signs or symbols of objects. The Chinese are merely interested in the inter-relations between the different signs, without being bothered by the substance underlying them.

Chinese and Western thought, says Chang, differ in their basic attitudes:

In putting a question about anything, it is characteristic of Western mentality to ask "What is it?" and then later "How should one react to it?" The Chinese mentality does not emphasize the "what" but rather the "how." Western thought is characterized by the "what-priority attitude," Chinese by the "how-priority attitude." Neglect of the "what" accounts for the neglect or absence of epistemology in China. That Chinese thought always centers on human affairs while neglecting nature may thus be accounted for.

The fourth opinion is that of Georges Margouliès, a historian and translator of Chinese literature. Writing in 1943, Margouliès affirms that Chinese is superior to all the West-

138

ern languages. Concepts in Chinese retain their integrity, he says. Because a concept does not change in form, the Chinese thinks of it as absolute and abstract, while the Westerner must modify his words in keeping with grammatical rules. The Chinese language therefore has a great power of objectivity and abstraction, while languages with changing forms are more subjective, concrete, limited, and relative.

The language of Westerners is egocentric, Margouliès says, and this causes difficulties in abstract thought. As a result of the weakness of its speech forms, the West has turned to mathematics. In China, the development of mathematics has been less important because the ideographic script and isolating structure of the language had already established modes of thought analogous to the mathematical. But because of its rationality and distance from emotion, Chinese is not as good as a Western language for religious thinking.

The fifth opinion is that of Yuen Ren Chao, the founder of modern linguistics in China. Writing in 1959, he finds that the logic in Chinese is like that in other languages. "Like the logic of other cultures, Chinese logic operates by way of affirmation and negation, particular and universal assertion, categorical conclusion and hypothetical imperative, etc. . . . While aiming to find out how Chinese logic operates, we shall probably end up with finding how logic operates in Chinese." There are differences, however. "Rather than affirmation and negation, Chinese logic operates really with truth or falsehood, stated in the form of agreement or disagreement." Although, speaking generally, the Chinese language restricts logic too much—that is, its forms are too specific, it suits modern, post-Aristotelian formal logic quite well.

The sixth, last opinion is that of Joseph Needham, the embryologist who, in his *Science and Civilization in China*, the volumes of which are still being published, has been revealing the whole scientific-technological dimension of Chinese culture. Like Fryer, he is equipped to grasp the adequacy of Chinese for contemporary science, but he is also able to judge the clarity of ancient technical Chinese. As expressed in 1961, this is his opinion:

The inhibiting influence of the ideographic language has been grossly over-rated. It has proved possible to draw up large glossaries of definable technical terms used in ancient and medieval times for all kinds of things and ideas in science and its applications. At the present day, the language is no impediment to contemporary scientists. If the social and economic factors in Chinese society had permitted or facilitated the rise of modern science there as well as in Europe, then already 300 years ago the language would have been made suitable for scientific expression. The classical language had great capacity. We do not remember any well-considered instance in which we have been seriously in doubt as to what was intended by a classical or medieval Chinese author dealing with a scientific or technical subject, provided that the text was not too corrupt, and that the description was sufficiently full. The general tendency was, of course, to make the descriptions too laconic.

This is not the place nor do I have the knowledge to make a serious analysis of the six opinions I have cited. But I do want to summarize the points that seem right to me, and to add one or two that have not been mentioned. The remarks I am about to make are my own unauthenticated conclusions, and I put them down simply in order not to evade thinking about the subject. For whatever they are worth, here they are:

1. We know that the Chinese developed some forms of algebra to about the level of the Renaissance, which is also, perhaps, the level of their later technology. We must assume that their language was adequate to their science and technology. We have no good grounds, therefore, to suppose the Chinese unable to think scientifically or technologically, or to blame their language for any failure to develop further.

2. Formal logic must be built into the Chinese language as into every other. It must, that is, have constant structures. Otherwise it would be impossible to understand. In principle, then, its formal structures could be abstracted from it and turned into a sort of mathematics. How different the logic of Chinese may be from that of our own languages, I cannot say, inasmuch as the logic of Chinese is hardly known as yet. It appears to be poorly suited to Aristotelian logic, the first to develop in the Western tradition. Yet I suspect that the logic of Chinese is not very

140

different from ours, and my reason is that all languages fill much the same basic purposes for much the same kind of human creatures.

3. Chinese fits the linguistic idea of an advanced language, efficient at making statements that are not bound to particular circumstances. In the fixity of its units, whose order changes to express changes in meaning, it is already in the state toward which the Indo-European languages, especially English, are tending.

4. But literary Chinese is allusive, context-bound, ambiguous or ambivalent, and analytically incomplete in ways that justify regarding it as relatively esthetic rather than logical. It is allusive and context-bound in that it contains innumerable hints at more or less classic texts. Unless the hints are understood, the meanings are incomplete. In actual use it is often an erudite allusion-and-pun game. Its skeleton of logic is therefore relatively less dominant than in ordinary Western writing. It is ambiguous, furthermore, because expressed in parallelisms, analogies, and paradoxical-sounding combinations of opposites, all of which allow a wide range of interpretations. That is to say, it does not make use of a sufficient number of sufficiently organized logical constants to be clear.

Briefly, the ground for the different judgments of Chinese is this: Chinese has a fixed, objective skeleton, made up of unchanging symbols, their fixed grammatical distinctions reduced to a minimum, and their function depending largely on position. This fixed skeleton is minimal. It is a drastic shorthand to be expanded associatively by each reader. In addition, each symbol in the skeletal symbol-chain is a node for traditional and, no doubt, personal associations. Chinese is therefore a good language for subjective or inner speech. This subjective, inner speech parallels or shadows or intersects the objective, external meanings. In other words, Chinese, as it has been actually used, has been relatively more developed as an esthetic than as a scientific language.

Let me expand on this last point with some guesses on the visual and gestural qualities of Chinese. Chinese characters are assigned traditional, often mistaken origins, which are pictorial or symbolic. There is therefore a tendency, stronger and more complex than in the alphabetic languages, to make visual associations with words. But the associations, or the empathies, also involve the arm, because the motion required to write the characters remains visible in them. The writing is composed of strokes, each with its permanently visible direction, velocity, and weakening and intensification.

Both gesturally and imaginatively, then, literary Chinese is like Chinese painting, especially of the scholar-type. As gesture and imagination it is in some ways more complex than as logic. By this I mean that as logic Chinese tends to express *all* relationships by coordination or antithesis. It finds complex subordination and superordination hard to express. It hardly has our subordinate clauses or complex relations of tenses. But complex subordination and super-ordination are expressed in the gestural structures of writing and painting. To say this is to repeat that the Chinese have got further in poetic analogies and inky motions than in formal logic and theoretical science.

Let me try to explain myself again, in another way. Chinese writing began as a specialized form of drawing. It had an aura of magic, the strokes of the drawing retaining the life of whatever they recorded. Writing remained somewhat magical. Society was upheld by its presence and its meanings. To show it disrespect was even, in the context of traditional cosmology, to threaten the universal order. However faintly, to write was to prolong the gestures of the universe. Maybe this old magical tradition did not make much difference to the later Chinese. But surely writing was taken to constitute something of a man's worth. It was regarded as his inner being made manifest to be appreciated and internalized by others.

Pattern in Nature, Language, and Art

Like painting, and like the calligraphy inseparable from it, writing was therefore considered to be a projection of the universal pattern of things. Liu Hsieh (462–522), the great literary critic, used the word "pattern," *wen*, for "literature"

142

as well. Originating in the Great Ultimate, the pattern of nature, he said, expressed itself in our moral, plastic, musical, and linguistic patterns, for man, the mind of the universe, spoke the universe aloud:

Wen, or pattern, is a very great power indeed. It is born together with heaven and earth. Why do we say this? Because all color-patterns are mixed of black and yellow [heaven and earth as colors], and all shape-patterns are differentiated by round and square [heaven and earth as shapes]. The sun and moon like two pieces of jade manifest their pattern of heaven; mountains and rivers in their beauty display the pattern of earth. These are, in fact, the pattern of *Tao* itself. And as one sees above the sparkling heavenly bodies, and below the manifold forms of earth, there is established a difference between high and low estate, giving rise to the two archetypal Forms [Yin and Yang]. Man, and man alone, forms with these the Great Trinity, and he does so because he alone is endowed with spirituality. He is the refined essence of the five elements —indeed the mind of the universe.

Now with the emergence of mind, language is created, and when language is created, writing appears. This is natural. When we extend our observations, we find that all things, both animals and plants, have patterns of their own. . . . The sculptured colors of clouds surpass paintings in their beauty, and the blossoms of plants depend on no embroiderers for their marvellous grace. Can these features be due to external adornment? No, they are all natural. Furthermore, the sounds of the forest wind blend to produce melody comparable to that of a reed pipe or lute, and the music created when a spring strikes upon a rock is as melodious as the ringing tone of a jade instrument or bell. Therefore, just as when nature expresses itself in physical bodies there is plastic pattern, so also, when it expresses itself in sound, there is musical pattern. Now if things which are devoid of consciousness express themselves so extremely decoratively, can that which is endowed with mind lack a pattern proper to itself?

The Interdependence
of Opposites:
Principle and
Matter-Energy

Pattern, to the Chinese, has always implied the interdependence of opposites. Chinese words are themselves often paired antithetical concepts—size, for example, is "large-small." Chinese logic, we have said, is based on the principle of correlative duality. Chinese poetry is saturated with careful antitheses. It seems that everything must have its opposite. In an anthology edited by Chu Hsi we find this stated quite explicitly:

> Some one asked, "According to the Principle of Heaven and Earth, nothing exists in isolation but everything necessarily has its opposite. As there is activity, there is necessarily tranquillity, and as there is Yin, there is necessarily Yang, and so on, including expansion and contraction, rising and falling, and flourishing and decline. Has this been so from the beginning?"
> Chu Hsi answered, "It has been so from the beginning."

Of the antithetical pairs of concepts, there are perhaps two that dominate later Chinese philosophy. The first pair is Principle (*li*) and Matter-Energy (*ch'i*). The second is Knowledge (*chih*) and Action (*hsing*).

Traditionally, *li*, which I have translated Principle, was assumed to mean "veins in jade," and, as a verb, "to dress jade." This doubtful etymology aside, the word has a series of related meanings. To speak of the noun meanings alone, these are "order," "pattern," "organization," "reason," and "law." The translation, "principle," conveys that *li* is the principle of existence, which is both metaphysical and moral.

In many of its philosophical uses, *li* is like the Greek and medieval conceptions of "form" or "essence." At times it resembles the late medieval conception of "thisness" (*haecceitas*), which is supposed to make the object in which it resides, and from which it is inseparable, exactly what it is. "It will be found," says a text characterizing *li*, "that a thing must have a reason why it is as it is and a rule to which it should conform, which is what is meant by "principle!" Another text says, a little more explicitly, that *li* is "that by which a single thing is as it is." A third text adds that *li* is, "for example, that by which fire is hot and that by which water is cold."

To the Neo-Confucians, *li* was a single something that gave permanency in change and unity in plurality. "That a tree flowers in spring and fades in autumn," they said, "is a *permanent* principle. As for *permanent* flowering, there is no such principle; on the contrary, it would be a delusion. Now the Buddhists regard death as proof of *impermanence*. If there is death there is *regularity*; if there were no death, on the contrary, there would be *no regularity*." And as for unity in plurality, Chu Hsi explained, in an image, that the light of the moon is scattered on rivers and lakes and seen everywhere, yet the moon itself has not been split. In another passage, Chu Hsi repeated a series of questions and answers, to the same effect:

"How do you distinguish between *tao* and *li*?"
"*Tao* is path, while *li* are the lines."
"Like the grain in wood?"
"Yes."
"In that case there seems to be no difference."
"The word *tao* is all-embracing; the *li* are so many veins inside the *tao*."

Ch'i, the concept which is paired with *li*, is the "life-breath" of painting and, in the context of cosmology, "air," "ether," and "force." For Neo-Confucian metaphysics, such a translation as "matter-energy" or "material force" seems best. Like the Presocratics of ancient Greece and the Indian philosophers, the Chinese did not distinguish matter from energy.

The relationship between *li* and *ch'i* came to be conceived rather like that of form and matter in traditional European philosophy. *Li*, that is, was prior in importance, but normally could not exist in the absence of *ch'i*. As Chu Hsi explained:

Fundamentally Principle and Material Force cannot be spoken of as prior or posterior. But if we must trace their origin, we are obliged to say that Principle is prior. However, Principle is not a separate entity. It exists right in Material

145

Force. Without Material Force, Principle would have nothing to adhere to. As Material Force, there are the Five Agents (or Elements) of Metal, Wood, Water, and Fire. As Principle there are Humanity, Righteousness, Propriety, and Wisdom.*

As the last sentence implies, Chu Hsi was most interested in the moral implications of his doctrine. He used the pairing of *li* and *ch'i* to explain the joint presence in man of perfection and imperfection. Again like Plato, Aristotle, and the medieval philosophers of Europe, he assumed that the Principle was perfect, but that moral imperfection was the result of the imperfection of the Matter-Energy that made things different from one another. Chu Hsi therefore used the concept of Matter-Energy to explain the inequality between human beings, much as the concept of heredity may be used:

Our original nature [he said] is perfectly good, but if we do not discuss it along with physical nature, we shall not understand why some people are intelligent and others are stupid, and why some are strong while others are weak. Therefore the discussion is not complete. If we discuss only physical nature but not its source, although we know people are different in intelligence and strength, we shall not realize that in their source, which is perfectly good, they are not different. Therefore the discussion will not be intelligible. We must examine both before the discussion can become thorough.

Such a belief in *li* as everyone's perfectly good original nature might have led to a Rousseauistic sentimentalism. But the usual Neo-Confucian was nothing if not disciplined. He wanted, not to escape fate, but to make the most of it. As Chu Hsi said:

If one's moral character is not adequate to overcome Material Force, then there is nothing for him to do but to submit to Material Force as endowed by Heaven. If one's moral character is adequate to overcome Material Force, however, then what he received from the endowment is all. . . . The cases in which Material Force cannot be altered are life, death, and longevity and brevity of life, for these, and poverty and wealth, and

---

* I do not know why the translation I have used here omits the fifth Agent or Element, which is Earth, or in the immediately following list, omits Faithfulness.

honor and humble station all depend on Material Force. On the other hand, the practice of righteousness between the ruler and his ministers and the exercise of humanity between father and son are matters of fate. But there is also Man's Nature. The superior man (we read in Mencius) does not say they are matters of fate. They must proceed from oneself, not from fate.

Together with this partial resignation and with this acceptance that history was cyclical, that is, largely a matter of fate, the Neo-Confucians—influenced, I assume, by the Buddhists—saw the moral and metaphysical universe as basically one, and the separations between things as the result of artificial obstructions. In the words of Chu Hsi:

The operation of the Principle of the mind penetrates all as blood circulates and reaches the entire body. If there is a single thing not yet entered, the reaching is not yet complete, and there are things not yet embraced. This shows that the mind still excludes something. For selfishness separates and obstructs, and consequently one and others stand in opposition. This being the case, even those dearest to us may be excluded. Therefore the mind that leaves something outside is not capable of uniting itself with the mind of Heaven.

The Neo-Confucian Attack on Buddhism

The Neo-Confucians, Chu Hsi among them, regarded Buddhism as the enemy. Its ideology was meant to detach a man from his family and community and from his earthly concerns in general. The Buddhist's ideal was meditation and, distantly, nirvana. The monk, the monastery, and the Buddhist leadership became new foci of loyalty, competing with the old. This threatened the dissolution of the traditional family and the weakening of all Confucian principles. The Neo-Confucians countered the threat by assimilating everything possible that made Buddhism attractive, its emphasis on intuitive understanding, its humanitarianism, and, perhaps above all, its view of the world as a system. The primacy of *li* and its penetration through the body of the world, and the hope to overcome the human and cosmic obstructions caused by selfishness, all suggest

147

the emphases of later Buddhism. But this assimilation of attitude was coupled with an attack. Instead of joining *li* and *ch'i*, the Buddhists, it was said, disjoined them. They neglected facts, history, and moral responsibilities:

Since the Buddhist doctrine spread in China like fire, many Confucianists, who have not been able to look through the gate of the school of the Sage, have already been attracted to it and drowned in it together with the Buddhists. They consider Buddhism as the great Way. Consequently, its vulgarism has extended throughout the world, so that good and bad people, the intelligent and the stupid, men and women, and servants, all have become accustomed to believing in it. . . . Before understanding the mind of the Sage, they have already concluded that the manifestation of his mind in historical facts need not be investigated, and, before understanding the purpose of the superior man, they have already concluded that it is not necessary to devote oneself to the concrete expressions of that mind. That is why human relations have not been clearly understood, the Principle of things has not been clearly comprehended, government has been neglected, and morality has become a chaos. Strange doctrines fill the ear. From above, there have been no rules of propriety to prevent their treachery. From below, there has been no study to examine their defects. For 1,500 years they have all come from the Buddhist school.

The Neo-Confucians charged that the Buddhists not only neglected their human duties, but tried to commit the impossible act of fleeing from the world in which they continued to exist:

Buddhism has the doctrine that one should leave the family and the world. One cannot really leave the family; but of course it is possible for them to run away from it by not treating their parents as parents. As for the world, how can one leave it? To leave the world can only mean no longer having the sky above you and the earth below you. None the less they drink when they are thirsty and eat when they are hungry, have the sky above them and the earth below.

Chu Hsi was ready to admit that the Buddhists were morally serious. But he insisted that they were fundamentally different, too interested in the transcendental, too little in the empirical. "They differ," he said, "from us Confucianists. They are fundamentally impatient, and there-

148

fore want to do away with everything. We Confucianists treat existing things as existent and nonexisting things as nonexistent. All we want is that when we handle things we shall manage them in the correct way."

The interaction between Neo-Confucianism and Buddhism could extend even to humor. Zen Buddhism was attacked with a flash of Zenlike humor: "The Zen doctrine of leaving the world is like closing one's eyes and not seeing one's nose; the nose is there of itself."

The Interdependence of Opposites: Knowledge and Action

Neo-Confucianism and Buddhism, it appears, can be understood, Chinese fashion, as an antithetical and interdependent pair. The increasing influence of Buddhism on Neo-Confucianism led to a stress on a concept pair that may be translated "knowledge-action" (*chih-hsing*). The problem conveyed by the pair is the universal and perennial one, argued explicitly in the West from the time of Socrates: if you know what is right, does this knowledge necessarily lead to right acts?

In Chinese thought, the doctrine of the unity of knowledge and action is associated with Wang Yang-ming, also known as Wang Shou-jen (1472–1529). Wang was a scholar, reformer, and successful military leader. His doctrine was a protest against the externality and the essential pettiness he saw in official life. He said:

The reason the world is not in order is because superficial writing is growing and concrete practice is declining. People advance their own opinions, valuing what is novel and strange, in order to mislead the common folks and gain fame. They merely confuse people's intelligence and dull people's senses, so that people devote much of their time and energy in order to compete in conventional writing and flowery compositions in order to achieve fame; they no longer remember that there are such deeds as honoring the fundamental, valuing truth, and returning to simplicity and purity.

These words were aimed at the doctrines and school of Chu Hsi, which had long since become official. Wang rejected Chu's "investigation of things," which meant, not empirical science, but a conventionalized moral analysis. This analysis led too often to the same conclusion, the one most natural to entrenched officialdom: be loyal and obey your superiors of every sort and rank. The result, Wang believed, was moral corruption overlaid by verbal piety. Knowledge separated from action, he said, was not knowledge at all: "Knowledge in its genuine and earnest aspect is action, and action in its intelligent and discriminating aspect is knowledge. At bottom the task of knowledge and action cannot be separated. Knowledge is what constitutes action and unless it is acted upon cannot be called knowledge."

Because he considered knowledge and action to be one, Wang hoped to influence people to think only pure thoughts. But he was impressive because he demanded, and exemplified in his life, the equivalence between moral ideals and moral deeds:

Suppose we say that so-and-so knows filial piety and so-and-so knows brotherly respect. They must have actually practiced filial piety and brotherly respect before they can be said to know them. It will not do to say that they know filial piety and brotherly respect simply because they know them in words. Or take one's knowledge of pain. Only after one has experienced pain can one know pain. The same is true of cold or hunger. How can knowledge and action be separated? This is the original substance of knowledge and action, which have not been separated by selfish desires. In teaching people, the Sage insisted that only this can be called knowledge. Otherwise, this is not yet knowledge. That is a serious and practical business.*

* Wang is obviously speaking in a contemporary voice. Compare what he says with the following passage on the function of the academic:
"Isn't the academic's function to 'think' rather than 'act'? . . . The question invokes the conventional dichotomy between 'thinking' and 'doing' which seems to be an occupational disease among academics. The reply to it is, I think, to ask what the sense is of treating 'thinking' and 'doing' as separate if not indeed incompatible activities. Analysis and discussion, where they are politically relevant, become political *acts*—and it is this that we have specified as the peculiar social responsibility of intellectuals. To think, to speak, to teach, to write: all these *are* forms of doing

In his approach to the serious and practical business of education, Wang showed what seems to me an un-Chinese generosity toward schoolchildren. He must have remembered his own childhood clearly. He sounds, strangely enough, like Montaigne:

Generally speaking, it is the nature of young boys to love to play and to dislike restriction. Like plants beginning to sprout, if they are allowed to grow freely, they will develop smoothly. If twisted and interfered with, they will wither and decline. In teaching young boys today, we must make them lean toward rousing themselves so that they will be happy and cheerful at heart, and then nothing can check their development. . . . However, in recent generations the teachers of youngsters merely supervise them every day as they recite phrases and sentences and imitate civil service examination papers. They stress restraint and discipline instead of directing their pupils in the practice of propriety. They emphasize intelligence instead of nourishing goodness. They beat the pupils with a whip and tie them with ropes, treating them like prisoners. The youngsters look upon their school as a prison and refuse to enter. They regard their teachers as enemies and do not want to see them. They avoid this and conceal that in order to satisfy their desire for play and fun. They pretend, deceive, and cheat in order to indulge in mischief and meanness. They become negligent and inferior, and daily degenerate. Such education drives them to do evil. How can they be expected to do good?

Wang accepted and accentuated the Chinese belief in the unity of nature and man. The great man, he said, regards the world as one family and the country as one man, whereas the small man loses and destroys humanity:

[Wang says, "I want people to understand that when a thought is aroused it is already action"]. They ought properly to be seen as integral components of action and as an indispensable part of the political process. Without going any further, an academic may help make the life of his society richer and nobler. But what if he does go further? If a man's thought should carry over into more overt forms of action . . . are we to regard it as somehow automatically debased? Surely not. For in a healthy personality, thought and action merge gracefully along a single spectrum and there is no artificial barrier that prevents a man from undertaking some task of leadership or organization in order to realize in fact what his understanding tells him must be done." T. Roszak, "On Academic Delinquency," in T. Roszak, *The Dissenting Academy*, London, Penguin Books & Chatto & Windus, 1969, pp. 36–37 (American edition: New York, Random House, 1967).

When his mind is aroused by desires and obscured by selfishness, compelled by greed for gain and fear of harm, and stirred by anger, he will destroy things, kill members of his own species, and will do everything. In extreme cases he will even slaughter his own brothers, and the humanity that forms one body will disappear completely.

In contrast, the great man will rid himself of selfish desires and restore his oneness with the world, for "everything from ruler, minister, husband, wife, and friends to mountains, rivers, spiritual beings, birds, animals, and plants, should be truly loved in order to realize my humanity that forms one body with them, and then my clear character will be completely manifested."

Wang, with his stress on intuition, unselfishness, nonattachment, and universal oneness was accused of being a Buddhist in disguise. But in the crucial matter, the conviction that society was valuable in itself, he was a genuine Neo-Confucian, and the comprehensive love he advocated fell a little short of including the Buddhists. They were selfish he said, and so, moderately but resolutely, he opposed them:

Buddhism claims to be free from attachment to phenomenal things but actually the opposite is the case. We Confucians seem to be attached to phenomenal things but in reality the opposite is true. . . . In all cases, because the relationships between ruler and minister, father and son, and husband and wife involve attachment to phenomena, they have to escape from them. We Confucians accept the relationship between father and son and fulfill it with the humanity it deserves. We accept the relationship between ruler and minister and fulfill it with the righteousness it deserves. We accept the relationship between husband and wife and fulfill it with the attention it deserves. When have we been attached to these relations?

A Comparison:
Wang Yang-ming
and John Dewey

The initial implausibility of a comparison may be what makes it interesting. It appears implausible that Wang Yang-ming, the fifteenth-century Neo-Confucian, should be like John Dewey, the twentieth-century American Pragmatist. If I say, as is true, that there is some likeness in their philosophical backgrounds, this statement, as well, is initially implausible. I think that the two were basically different in some ways, yet they were alike, not culturally, but personally, in assuming the unity of knowledge and action and the related continuity, as Dewey put it, of mind with nature. Let me explain.

When Wang spoke of unity, the terms he used were, even in translation, clearly Chinese: "One body," he said, and "one family." "The great man," he said, "regards Heaven, Earth, and the myriad things as one body. He regards the world as one family and the country as one person. As to those who make a cleavage between objects and distinguish between the self and others, they are small men."

Dewey used another terminology, that of "organic development." He said:

The doctrine of organic development means that the living creature is a part of the world, sharing its vicissitudes and fortunes, and making itself secure in its precarious dependence only as it intellectually identifies itself with the things about it. If the living, experiencing being is an intimate participant in the activities of the world to which it belongs, then knowledge is a mode of participation, valuable in the degree in which it is effective. It cannot be the ideal view of an unconcerned spectator.

Both Wang and Dewey, we see, had the feeling of being part of a greater world-organism, which must be acknowledged in our thoughts and acts. And because thoughts and acts were identical, both Wang and Dewey concluded that learning could not be intellectual alone, cut off from action. Wang said, typically:

To learn archery, one must hold out the bow, fix the arrow to the bow, and take aim. To learn writing, one must lay out paper, take the brush, hold the inkwell, and dip the brush in it. In all the world, nothing can be considered learning that does not involve action. Thus the very beginning of learning is already action.

To this text there are many approximately equivalent ones of Dewey. His devotion to the experimental method made him different from Wang, but he was equally reluctant "to call anything knowledge except where our activity has actually produced certain physical changes in things." The activity ought not to be merely utilitarian. It ought to have integrity. "To be earnest in practice," Wang said, "means to be genuine and sincere." Dewey used the term "singlemindedness," and explained:

What the word is here intended to convey is *completeness* of interest, unity of purpose; the absence of suppressed but effectual ulterior aims for which the professed aim is but a mask. It is the equivalent of mental integrity. Absorption, engrossment, full concern with the subject matter for its own sake, nurture it. Divided interest and evasion destroy it.

Having equated learning with action, both philosophers thought it began in active doubt. Wang said:

In learning, one cannot help doubts. Therefore one inquires. To inquire is to learn; it is to act. As there is still doubt, one thinks. To think is to learn; it is to act. As there is still doubt, one sifts. To sift is to learn; it is to act. As the sifting is clear, the thinking careful, the inquiry accurate, and the study competent, one goes further and continues his effort without a stop.

A similar and typical text of Dewey enumerates "the general features of a reflective experience," which include doubt, a tentative interpretation, and a careful survey. Unlike Wang, Dewey is thinking of a hypothesis being tested for future use. This air of modern science is foreign to Wang, but the concatenated, energizing doubt is not.

It is worth noting that Wang's followers split into competing groups, all overshadowed during the seventeenth century by the prevailing antimystical tendency and the empiricism that rested on textual research, philology, and archeology. But in Japan, and in China of the late nineteenth and early twentieth centuries, Wang's philosophy of sincerity and action influenced the revolutionaries, among them Sun Yat-sen and Liang Ch'i-ch'ao. Its revival coincided in part with the influence of John Dewey, who lectured in China from 1919 to 1921. It is possible to speculate that his hearers found him convincing because his message coincided in part with the one that had already been delivered by Wang Yang-ming.

Puritanism,
Censorship

Neo-Confucianism has so far been presented as a set of philosophical abstractions. But it had its practical side. Not only did it conduct polemics against Buddhism, but it had a generally censorious, puritanical, and antilibertarian effect. It insisted more on the subordination of woman to man and subject to ruler. Bodily and especially sexual functions came to be regarded as more shameful. Books written in the spirit of later Confucianism exacerbate the spirit of early Confucianism and hide sexuality; and paintings, to be decent, are of flowers or of meditative scholars, in or out of landscapes, but not of anything openly sexual. The son is taken to revere his father, and decent literature finds it impossible to hint at any difficulty between them. The possibility of sexual attraction between mother and son is completely taboo.

What was officially forbidden continued, of course, to exist. Pornographic art might be cultivated here and there. Confucian scruples might be directed against the government. But official Neo-Confucianism had a heavy hand. This may be illustrated by the literary inquisition of Ch'ien-lung, the model prince of an earlier chapter and the persecutor of the present one.

In imitation of his father, Ch'ien-lung decided to allow only the official interpretation of the classics. When the situation was ripe, he instituted a literary inquisition. The tests he applied were these:

Is the book in question antidynastic or in any other way rebellious? Does it insult previous dynasties that might be assumed to be ancestral to the present one, the Ch'ing? Does the book concern the northern or northwestern frontiers or military or naval defences? Does it contain the writings of certain suspect authors? Does it contain unorthodox opinions on the Confucian canon? Does it have an unliterary style? Does it give a wrong account of certain traditional historic events? Does it concern suspect political groups?

A single case may be taken to symbolize the inquisition. One Hsieh Chi-shih, an important official, came to the

Emperor in person to request that the governor of Honan be impeached for misuse of funds. The Emperor refused, Hsieh insisted. The Emperor, enraged, handed Hsieh over to the Board of Punishments. While having Hsieh beaten, the President of the Board asked him why he had been so disrespectful. Hsieh answered that he had learned from Confucius and Mencius that a man was disloyal if he did not speak out against evil.

Hsieh was banished. When, three years later, he was accused of having slandered Chu Hsi in a commentary, he was imprisoned for a while, and an edict was issued, saying:

I hear that the commentaries of Hsieh Chi-shih on the canon have been published and spread abroad; that in large measure the author's comments give free rein to his own fancies and set forth views which are outrageous, opposed to those formulated by Ch'eng and Chu. Hitherto our students and scholars have hewed to the line and have not made much over petty differences and similarities between the words and expression of the text. Now the ancients wrote books in great profusion. Naturally in their writings occur occasional points open to criticism. Of what good is it to later individuals if they pick flaws in the writers of the past, whether correct or not in their flaw-finding? Cheng-tsu [Ch'ien-lung's father], moreover, made Chu Hsi one of the ten sages, and especially singled him out for veneration. In all China there is no one who does not regard him as one to pattern after.

But the school of Hsieh Chi-shih express different opinions, looking upon each other as models. I fear that men without knowledge will be unsettled by their teaching, and that there will arise variant modes of thought and behavior. I have not so far made a crime out of the utterances of men, but this matter is of too great significance.

It is pleasant to record that Hsieh nevertheless rose, under the next Emperor, to be a high official again.

The thoroughness of Ch'ien-lung's censorship may be judged by a proclamation he sent on August 11, 1778, to his officials:

Although censorable volumes have been sent up in numerous batches, they do not represent all, I fancy. Some must yet remain, possibly in very poor homes in the remote countryside, where the inhabitants had no chance of hearing my commands.

156

Such a proclamation would go out to the chief administrators, and they, in turn, would issue their proclamations —the following, for example, issued in 1778 by the lieutenant-governor of Chekiang:

In case you find that you have the books the titles of which are given in the *Indexes*, immediately deliver up the books, and let the aforesaid department and district educational commissioners promptly give notice of the fact to the provincial office, which in turn will confide despatch to Peking to a special deputy, for destruction.

So do you each and every literatus, member of the gentry, and commoner make the most meticulous kind of search in old cases for books and in travelling boxes. No matter whether they are broken sets or fragmentary copies, deliver up everything. Let there be no slightest thing left concealed, that you may avoid committing wrong. Tremble and obey, and do not disregard this.

"It was a brave Chinese," we are told, "who dared withhold a book. We have the record of one such at least, and he was sentenced to one hundred blows and exile for a period of three years." The Index of the Emperor listed 2,320 books for complete suppression, 342 for partial suppression, and three for the correction of a few words. It is impossible to know how much of Chinese literature was lost during the fifteen years of the inquisition, but the loss was surely great.

A Chinese
Conclusion

The literary inquisition was harsh. In Chinese life and thought there was a good deal of harshness that does not appear on a first, more romantic view. The alternation of humane and harsh has characterized every subject we have taken up, and sometimes it has been less an alternation than an entanglement of one in the other. Is it possible to speak of the Chinese in one breath, summarize their contrary qualities, and, in the image of the third-century critic, Lu Chi, "enclose boundless space in a square foot of paper"?

We can, I suppose, adopt one of the philosophical attitudes of the Chinese themselves and refuse to reach a conclusion. This attitude can be charming or exasperating—the reaction depends on how badly one wants to decide. The Chinese, as we have often noticed, were ambivalent, and the reaching of definite conclusions might only have made the ambivalence more painful. We of course share a good deal of this ambivalence, as we share the Chinese difficulty in uniting knowledge and action.

There is something we can add, which may have become evident in various ways. The hero of the Chinese, their philosopher-sage, was not the self-crucifying genius that we have learned to honor. In saying this I remember the Confucian conscience that might lead a man to sacrifice his life. I remember Ssu-ma Ch'ien. Yet the Chinese ideal was a smooth kind of man, as responsible as easy, as active as still. He caressed beautiful stones and, in the right circumstances, women. He was a healed Chinese intellectual, not separated from himself, from others, or from the universe.

Can we imagine him more closely? Let me try a moment to speak in his voice. I am, I say for him, slightly immortal. My immortality is not by means of a Western-style, disembodied soul, but by my ability to become internal to the landscape. I state and establish my existence, my "Therefore I am," in two equivalent styles of nostalgia, that of poetry and that of mountains-and-water. I live my life in obligations, but also, less obviously, in my shyness of them and my homesickness for infancy. Resolutely correct on the outside, I am sadly, humorously easy on the inside. Everything there, internally, is a random walk, with no goal but the absence of one. Goalless, I can rejoin all Being, that is to say, I can become reciprocal with the universe again. This goalless effort is my vocation.

> There is joy in this vocation; all sages esteem it.
> We struggle with Non-being to force it to yield Being; we knock upon Silence for an answering Music.
> We enclose boundless space in a square foot of paper; we pour out a deluge from the inch-space of the heart.
> Language spreads wider and wider; thought probes deeper and deeper.

The fragrance of delicious flowers is diffused; exuberant profusion of green twigs is budding.
A laughing wind will fly and whirl upward; dense clouds
will arise from the Forest of Writing Brushes.

Now, at the end, I do not want to translate this translation any further or to conclude in a more definite way. I
will not try to answer why, if he wants to be smooth, the
apprentice-sage must struggle. I will point out, however,
that in the Chinese original, the "square foot of paper" is
a length of silk, and also that the Forest of Writing Brushes
refers to the Imperial Academy. We and they, the Chinese,
are so far apart that we can communicate only with words
and pictures. This communication is difficult, but sometimes easier than we can accept. Here, at the end, we
should not allow ourselves to say anything very clear. In
the end, we cannot afford to be either careless or solemn.

BIBLIOGRAPHY

The bibliography that follows is, all things considered, quite short. I have chosen these books because they are up-to-date introductions or because they strike me as especially revealing or pleasurable. Further suggestions for reading may be found in the *Sources of Quotations*.

First, a number of general books. If I were confined to a single book for a serious student, I would choose *Sources of Chinese Tradition*, compiled by W. T. de Bary, Wing-tsit Chan, and B. Watson, New York, Columbia University Press, 1960. This anthology of nearly a thousand pages is distinguished by intelligent introductions and good translations. Philosophy, government, history, and religion are represented in it, and the concluding section, "China and the New World," is on the late nineteenth and twentieth centuries.

L. C. Goodrich's *A Short History of the Chinese People*, 3rd ed., New York, Harper & Row, 1959, shows not only the brevity proclaimed in its title, but also a strong interest in Chinese culture, including technology and science. *East Asia: The Great Tradition*, by E. O. Reischauer and J. K. Fairbank, Boston, Houghton Mifflin Co., 1960, is fuller and includes chapters on the related cultures of Korea and Japan. It is now often thought to be the best introductory history of China. It is followed by a companion volume, *East Asia: The Modern Transformation*.

M. Loewe, *Imperial China: The Historical Background to the Modern Age*, London, Allen & Unwin, 1966, gives an interesting description of Chinese government, culture, economy, and social life. J. Gernet, *Daily Life in China*, London, Allen & Unwin, 1962, is the translated work of a French Sinologist. Centered on the time, the later thirteenth century, just before the Mongol invasions, it begins with city life, and goes on from society, housing, clothing, cooking, and the life cycle, to a concluding portrait of China.

For a reliable history of China from the seventeenth century and on, see I. C. Y. Hsü, *The Rise of Modern China*, New York, Oxford University Press, 1970. It "conveys primarily a Chinese view of the evolution of modern China, reinforced by the fruits of Western and Japanese scholarship."

For Chapter 1, *Rulers and Sons*, T'ung-Tsu Ch'ü, *Law and Society in Traditional China*, The Hague, Mouton & Co., 1965. This is learned, well-documented, tough-minded, and filled with interesting examples, some of which I have used. S. van der Sprenkel, *Legal Institutions in Manchu China*, London, The Athlone Press, University of London, 1962, 1966, is a good, sociologically oriented introduction. To see how China looked to curious sixteenth-century Europeans, read *China in the 16th Century: The Journals of Matthew Ricci*, translated by L. J. Gallagher, from the Latin version of Trigault, New York, Random House, 1953. For the nineteenth century, Kung-chuan Hsiao's *Rural China, Imperial China in the Nineteenth Century*, Seattle, University of Washington, 1960, retains the feeling of the life it studies. Although a scholarly piece of work, it is enlivened by many illustrative incidents and quotations. The picture it draws is of a self-defeating imperial government, the docility of its subjects paid for by their increasing inability to cope with their harsh environment.

An objective and yet reasonably intimate sense of recent Chinese life is given by the books of two American anthropologists of Chinese origin: M. C. Yang, in *A Chinese Village*, New York, Columbia University Press, 1945, and F. L. K. Hsu, in *Under the Ancestor's Shadow*, New York, Columbia University Press, 1948. R. J. Lifton's *Thought Reform and the Psychology of Totalism*, reprinted by Penguin Books, 1967, is an insightful and sometimes terrifying book of quite another sort, in which the old social relations are clarified by means of the prolonged attack leveled against them by the Chinese Communists.

For Chapter 2, *Artists*, there are sumptuous books of reproductions. Most of them may be hard to find; but J. Cahill, *Chinese Painting*, Geneva, Skira, 1960, which is easily available, combines a knowledgeable text with well-reproduced illustrations. O. Siren, *Chinese Painting: Leading Masters and Principles*, 7 vols., London, Lund Humphries, 1956–58, is, in contrast, an encyclopedic survey in seven volumes. Its numerous illustrations, almost all in black and white, are made by a collotype process that is better for sharpness of detail than for range of tones. Siren's *The Chinese on the Art of Painting*, Peiping, Henri Vetch, 1936, recently reprinted in paperback, contains much the same texts as his history. Lin Yutang, in his similar anthology, *The Chinese Theory of Art*, London, Heinemann, 1967, makes fun of Siren and other Western translators. His text reads smoothly, but I have an unverified suspicion that this smoothness may sometimes be excessive. G. Rowley's *Principles of Chinese Paintings*, first published by Princeton University Press in 1947, is written by a scholar with unusual competence in the history of Western painting as well. His text, basically ahistorical, is eloquent at times and always clear. In *The Chinese Literati: Su Shih (1037–1101) to Tung Ch'i-ch'ang (1555–1636)*, Cambridge, Harvard University Press, 1971, S. Bush contends that the high evaluation of "amateur" art reflects the increasing dominance of the scholar-bureaucrats. The book contains many excerpts from the sources. For a study of Tung Ch'i-ch'ang's followers, the neo-orthodox opponents of eccentricity and individuality, see R. Whitfield, *In Pursuit of Antiquity*, The Art Museum, Princeton University, 1969. It contains many well-reproduced illustrations, often full-sized details.

There are many aspects of Chinese art that have hardly been explored as yet. These may have an interesting relation to Western art. One such aspect is explored by R. J. Maeda, in *The "Water" Theme in Chinese Painting*, Ascona, Switzerland, Artibus Asiae Publishers, 1971. Maeda's study contains fascinating illustrations of the styles in which water, whether calm or stormy, was depicted. *Welkulturen und moderne Kunst*, Munich, Bruckmann, 1972, contains brief, knowledgeable, plausibly illustrated sections on the influence of Chinese on Western art. An abbreviated English version of this extensive catalogue is available.

The most approachable of books on calligraphy is Chiang Yee, *Chinese Calligraphy*, 2nd ed., Cambridge, Harvard University Press, 1954. Written by an artist who practices what he describes, it has a subtle charm. Ch'en Chih-mai, *Chinese Calligraphers and Their Art*, Melbourne University Press, 1966, concentrates more on the history of the art.

Of all books on Chinese art, the one that identifies most with the Chinese art lover, with his analytical sensuousness and sensitivity to materials, mounts, and atmospheres, is R. H. van Gulik's *Chinese Pictorial Art as Viewed by the Connoisseur*, Rome, Instituto per il Medio ed Estreme Oriente, 1958. It contains actual samples of Chinese papers and silks. Not many copies of it were originally printed.

For literature, the first choice is C. Birch, *Anthology of Chinese Literature*, New York, Grove Press, 1965. J. J. Liu, *The Art of Chinese Poetry*, London, Routledge & Kegan Paul, 1962, is outstanding in that it is written by a man who grasps Western literature as well as Chinese. Arthur Waley, *The Life and Times of Po Chü-i*, London, Allen & Unwin, 1949, and Lin Yutang, *The Gay Genius: The Life and Times of Su Tungpo*, New York, John Day, 1947, will help readers to sense Chinese poets as individuals. David Hawkes, in *A Little Primer of Tu Fu*, London, Oxford University Press, 1967, gives a word-for-word and sound-for-sound analysis of the construction of Chinese poems. J. D. Frodsham, *The Poems of Li Ho 791–817*, London, Oxford University Press, 1970, translates a particularly striking poet. Of poetry anthologies, my favorite at the moment is A. C. Graham's *Poems of the Late T'ang*, Baltimore, Penguin Books, 1965. The English is untimid, and Graham transmits ambiguity by ambiguity. J. Scott (in collaboration with G. Martin), *Love and Protest: Chinese Poems from the Sixth Century B.C. to the Seventeenth Century A.D.*, London, Rapp & Whiting and André Deutsch, 1972, contains many poems not previously translated into English. These include prose-poems and poetry written in the vernacular. A quasi anthology and an anthology, by Burton Watson, are well worth reading for their fluent, sensitive translations and their well informed text. One is *Chinese Lyricism: Shih Poetry from the Second to the Twelfth Century*, New York, Columbia University Press, 1971. The other is *Chinese Rhyme-Prose: Poems in the Fu Form from the Han and Six Dynasties Period*, New York, Columbia University Press, 1971. The poems in the latter anthology are longer, more detailed, and more exuberant than those usually translated from the Chinese.

Translation has raised problems that are, of course, not completely soluble; but the freedom of contemporary English poetry gives translators from the Chinese fresh possibilities. As examples of the responsible exploitation of such possibilities I should like to cite two recent anthologies, E. Sackheim, . . . *the silent Zero in search of Sound*, New York, Grossman Publishers, 1968; and Wai-lim Yip, *Hiding the Universe: Poems by Wang Wei*, New York, Grossman Publishers, 1972. Both translators dislike the padding usually added in English and try to approximate the tautness of the original. Wai-lim Yip, incidentally, calls Wang Wei "the quietest poet in Chinese and perhaps in all literary history."

The bridge between traditional and modern poetry in China is described in J. C. Lin, *Modern Chinese Poetry: An Introduction*, Seattle, University of Washington Press, 1972.

Although I have hardly referred to novels, I should like to recommend C. T. Hsia's intelligent, forceful book, *The Classic Chinese Novel: A Critical Introduction*, New York, Columbia University Press, 1968.

In literary criticism, there is one surviving work, a poem by Lu Chi, that strikes me, as it has struck others, as a work of genius. I quote it at the end of this book and give the reference (in *Sources of Quotations*) to one of the three existing English translations. A second translation will be found on pages 204–14 of Birch's anthology, though without any notes.

The alchemical search for longevity, which I have mentioned in this chapter, is dealt with, from the alchemical standpoint, by N. Sivin, in *Chinese Alchemy: Preliminary Studies*, Cambridge, Harvard University Press, 1968. Sivin, who includes an annotated translation of an old Chinese treatise, is "a chemist by training and a historian of science by profession, who has at the same time a deep insight into the intricate ways of Far Eastern thought."

For Chapter 3, *Historians*, the general book is W. G. Beasley and E. G. Pulleyblank, *Historians of China and Japan*, London, Oxford University Press, 1961. De Bary's *Sources*, mentioned at the beginning of this bibliography, contains a number of translations from the historians. Burton Watson has translated two volumes of Ssu-ma Ch'ien and also has written a study of him. The names of his books will be found in *Sources of Quotations* to this chapter. To understand the odd genius of Chang Hsüeh-ch'eng, read D. S. Nivison, *The Life and Thought of Chang Hsüeh-ch'eng*, Stanford University Press, 1966.

For Chapter 4, *Cosmographers*, two books to begin with: Fung Yu-lan, *A Short History of Chinese Philosophy*, New York, Macmillan, 1948; and W.-T. Chan, *A Source Book in Chinese Philosophy*, Princeton University Press, 1963. Chan's translations are solid and are at their best, I think, for the Neo-Confucians, the philosophers who most concern us. Recent responsible translations of earlier classics are *Lao Tzu* and *Mencius*, both by D. C. Lau for Penguin Books, 1963, 1970. Although I refer only tangentially to Chuang Tzu, the most fantastic philosopher (or group of philosophers) in the world, it would be a pity to miss him (or them). B. Watson, whose English is fluent and whose scholarship, aided by Japanese commentaries, is exact, has done very handsomely in *The Complete Works of Chuang Tzu*, New York, Columbia University Press, 1968. Good as his translation generally is, it remains problematic in the more technically philosophical chapters. For another translation of one of these, with commentary, see A. C. Graham, "Chuang-tzu's Essay on Seeing Things as Equal," in the periodical, *History of Religions*, Chicago, Chicago University Press, 2–3, 1969–70, pp. 137–59. *Two Chinese Philosophers*, London, Lund Humphries, 1958, by A. C. Graham, shows what can be done by a Sinologist versed in Western philosophy.

For other matters dealt with in this chapter there is the multivolumed, still-uncompleted masterwork, J. Needham's *Science and Civilization in China*, London, Cambridge University Press, 1954 and on. This work, which marks an epoch in the study of Chinese culture, enlists the help of a whole crew of scholars and marries encyclopedism with vigor. Needham has written many essays on his subject, one of them in R. Dawson (ed.), *The Legacy of China*, London, Oxford University Press, 1964.

Chapter 5, *Philosophers*, naturally refers to the same sources as the preceding chapter. Of the simple, discursive introductions the best known is B. Karlgren, *Sound and Symbol in Chinese*, London, Oxford University Press, 1923; 2nd ed., 1962. Though still useful as an introduction, this book no longer reflects modern opinion. Perhaps P. Kratochvil, *The Chinese Language Today*, London, Hutchinson & Co., 1968, does so best; but this is a formidable little book unless one already knows something or has a teacher.

For a brief, compendious introduction to Chinese religion, some knowledge of which is essential for an understanding of Chinese philosophers, see D. H. Smith, *Chinese Religions from 1000 B.C. to the Present Day*, New York, Holt, Rinehart & Winston, 1968.

SOURCES OF QUOTATIONS

With minor exceptions, only the sources of the direct quotations are given here. These quotations are identified by the number of the page on which they begin and their first few words.

1

Rulers and Sons: The Empire of Filial Piety

5. "One may give up," A. H. Smith, *Proverbs and Common Sayings from the Chinese*, New York, Paragon Book Reprint Co. & Dover Publications, 1965, p. 305 (originally published by American Presbyterian Mission Press, 1914).
6. "Are not filial," Fung Yu-lan, *A History of Chinese Philosophy*, Princeton University Press, 1952, I, 361, note 1 (*Lun Yü* [*Analects*] I, 2).
6. "Now filial piety is," *ibid.*, p. 361 (*Hsiao Ching*).
6. "Filiality," H. S. Galt, *A History of Chinese Educational Institutions*, London, Probsthain, 1951, I, 108 (*Li Chi*, section *Chi I*).
6. "Men plant," Smith, *op. cit.*, p. 302 (clauses reversed).
6. "Girls too," *ibid.*, p. 303.
7. "Not to be angry," T'ung-Tsu Ch'ü, *Law and Society in Traditional China*, The Hague, Mouton & Co., 1965, p. 21.
7. "Ch'en Wen-hsuan," "Chiang Shao-hsien," *ibid.*, pp. 52–53.
8. "I have seen," *ibid.*, p. 61.
9. "The efficient," E. R. Hughes, *Chinese Philosophy in Classical Times*, London, Dent, Everyman's Library, 1954, p. 92 (*The Great Learning*, ch. 6).
9. Imperial Maxims, Kung-chuan Hsiao, *Rural China, Imperial Control in the Nineteenth Century*, Seattle, University of Washington Press, 1960, pp. 184–85.
10. "Don't let us," *ibid.*, p. 510.
12. "The Chinese nation," *The Travels and Controversies of Friar Domingo Navarrete, 1618–86*, in R. Dawson, *The Chinese Chameleon*, London, Oxford University Press, 1967, pp. 187–88.
13. "Most boys," M. C. Yang, *A Chinese Village, Taitou, Shan-*

tung Province, New York, Columbia University Press, 1945, pp. 145, 147.

14. "Prior to ascending," H. L. Kahn, "The Education of a Prince: The Emperor Learns His Roles," in A. Feuerwerker, R. Murphey, M. T. Wright, *Approaches to Modern Chinese History*, Berkeley, University of California Press, 1967, pp. 19–20.

16. "The entire kingdom," *China in the 16th Century: The Journals of Matthew Ricci: 1583–1610*, trans. L. J. Gallagher, New York, Random House, 1953, pp. 53–56.

18. "The prince," Kung-chuan Hsiao, *op. cit.*, p. 646, note 381.

19. "It is these," D. S. Nivison, "Protest Against Conventions and Conventions of Protest," in A. J. Wright, *The Confucian Persuasion*, Stanford, Stanford University Press, 1960, p. 197.

20. "Ch'i Hsien," Ping-ti Ho, *The Ladder of Success in Imperial China*, New York, Columbia University Press, 1962, pp. 272–73.

21. "The study of mathematics," *China in the 16th Century*, pp. 32–33.

22. "Those who," Ping-ti Ho, *op. cit.*, p. 130.

23. "If a rich," *ibid.*, p. 157.

24. "I remember," Shen Fu, *Chapters from a Floating Life*, trans. S. M. Black, London, Oxford University Press, 1960, p. 2.

24. "The Crazy Book Worm," *Chinese Ghost and Love Stories* (by P'u Sung-ling), trans. R. Quong, New York, Pantheon Books, 1946.

24. "I remember how," A. Waley, *Yuan Mei: Eighteenth Century Chinese Poet*, London, Allen & Unwin, 1956, pp. 165–66.

25. "All the much-idealized," R. J. Lifton, *Thought Reform and the Psychology of Totalism*, Baltimore, Penguin Books, 1967, p. 418.

25. "Save, save," *ibid.*, p. 425.

25. "Adultery," Tse-tsung Chow, "The Anti-Confucian Movement in Early Republican China," in A. J. Wright, *The Confucian Persuasion*, Stanford, Stanford University Press, 1960, p. 295.

2

Artists: Inspiration and Convention

29. Chinese classifications, B. March, *Some Technical Terms of Chinese Painting*, Baltimore, Waverly Press, 1935, pp. 15–17, 18–21.

32. "K'ai had," *The Biography of Ku K'ai-chih*, trans. Chen

Shih-hsiang, Berkeley, University of California Press, 1953. I have made slight verbal changes.

36. "With the blood," O. Siren, *Chinese Painting, Leading Masters and Principles*, London, Lund Humphries, 1956, I, 115.

37. "They seem to think," A. Waley, in R. Fry *et al.*, *Chinese Art*, New York, 1933, p. 71.

38. "The Great Message of Forests and Streams," in O. Siren, *The Chinese on the Art of Painting*, Peiping, 1936, pp. 43–52 (reprinted as paperback); Kuo Hsi, *An Essay on Landscape Painting*, trans. S. Sakanishi, London, John Murray, 1967, 1935; Lin Yutang, *The Chinese Theory of Art*, London, Heinemann, 1967, pp. 70–80.

40. "He took two," Siren, *op. cit.*, p. 134.

41. "Those who follow it," *ibid.*, p. 161.

42. "He would seat," Kuo Hsi, *An Essay on Landscape Painting*, p. 35.

44. "The Tao of painting," Siren, *Chinese Painting*, I, 136–37.

44. "When I was," Siren, *Chinese Painting*, II, 20.

46. "Having taken," my retrans. from G. Margouliès, *Anthologie raisonnée de la littérature chinoise*, Paris, 1948, pp. 385–88.

49. "The prices," Siren, *Chinese Painting*, II, 28.

49. "The artisan-painter," J. Levenson, "The Amateur Ideal in Ming and Early Ch'ing Society: Evidence from Painting," in J. K. Fairbank, *Chinese Thought and Institutions*, Chicago, University of Chicago Press, 1957, p. 138.

49. "Take eloquence," Verlaine, *Art Poétique*.

51. "The first lesson," Ch'en Chih-mai, *Chinese Calligraphers and Their Art*, Melbourne, Melbourne University Press, 1966, p. 192.

51. "Which are done by," Siren, *Chinese Painting*, II, 38.

52. "From examples," Chiang Yee, *Chinese Calligraphy*, 2nd ed., Cambridge, Harvard University Press, 1954, pp. 11–12.

53. "But one cannot," Siren, *The Chinese on the Art of Painting*, pp. 110–111.

54. "Only Ni Tsan," *ibid.*, p. 149.

55. "Someone has said," *ibid.*, p. 143.

56. Texture strokes, Mai-mai Sze, *The Way of Chinese Painting*, New York, Vintage Books, 1959, p. 134.

57. "In painting pictures," *ibid.*, pp. 127, 130.

57. Checklist, Wen Fong, *The Problem of Forgeries in Chinese Painting*, Ascona, Switzerland, Artibus Asiae, 1962 (from *Artibus Asiae*, Vol. XXV).

58. "If they, the curio," R. H. van Gulik, *Chinese Pictorial Art as Viewed by the Connoisseur*, Rome, Instituto Italiano per il Medio ed Estreme Oriente, 1958, p. 383.

59. "Found a perverse," R. H. van Gulik, *Sexual Life in Ancient China*, Leiden, Brill, 1961, p. 313.

59. "There has been," J. Cahill, *Chinese Painting*, Geneva, Skira, 1960, p. 172.

60. Shih-t'ao's essay, a too-free rendering; see Siren, *The Chinese on the Art of Painting*, pp. 184–88; Lin Yutang, *The Chinese Theory of Art*, pp. 140–43; V. Contag, *Die Beiden Steine*, Braunschweig, Germany, Hermann Klemm, 1950, pp. 57, 58.
61. "If, even," J. F. Cahill, "Confucian Elements in the Theory of Painting," in A. F. Wright, *The Confucian Persuasion*, Stanford, Stanford University Press, 1960, p. 132.
61. "Queerly tangled," Siren, *Chinese Painting*, II, 13.
61. "In his early years," *ibid.*, pp. 14–15.
62. "The problem," retrans. from *Aspects de la Chine*, Paris, Presses Universitaires de France, 1959; Cahill, *Chinese Painting*, p. 169.
62. Shih-ch'i's poem, Contag, *op. cit.*, pp. 50–51.
62. "War," *ibid.*, p. 8.
64. "What is the world," from G. Debon, *Li Tai-bo, Gedichte*, Stuttgart, Reclam, p. 137; on the P'eng, pp. 132–33.

3

Historians: The Men and Their Institutions

68. "Prior to the Three Dynasties," *Kuo Jo-Hsü's Experiences in Painting (An Eleventh Century History of Chinese Painting)*, trans. A. C. Soper, Washington, D.C., American Council of Learned Societies, 1951, p. 14.
68. "Had cast him off," "In tears," A. C. Graham, *Poems of the Late T'ang*, Baltimore, Penguin Books, 1965, pp. 119 (Li Ho), 99 (Li Ho).
69. "Miss Li," Po Hsing-chien, "The Story of Miss Li," trans. A. Waley, in C. Birch, *Anthology of Chinese Literature*, New York, Grove Press, 1965, p. 300.
69. "All things," H. Suyin, *The Crippled Tree*, London, Mayflower Books, 1968, pp. 30–31.
71. O future," *ibid.*, p. 41.
71. "The Secretary," D. C. Twitchett, "Chinese Biographical Writing," in W. G. Beasley and E. G. Pulleyblank, *Historians of China and Japan*, London, Oxford University Press, 1961, p. 104.
72. "Was born exactly," H. H. Frankel, "T'ang Literati: A Composite Biography," in A. F. Wright and D. Twitchett, *Confucian Personalities*, Stanford, Stanford University Press, 1962, p. 80 (on Ts'ui Hsin-ming).
72. "Renowned," "He was able," "He governed," "Boastful," "Possess," *ibid.*, pp. 81, 82, 83.
73. "Li Po," *The Works of Li Po*, trans. S. Obata, New York, Dutton, 1922, pp. 206–9.
74. "The whole empire," D. C. Twitchett, "Lu Chih (754–

805): Imperial Adviser and Court Official," in Wright and Twitchett, *op. cit.*, p. 96.

75. "As regards," C. Chang, *The Development of Neo-Confucian Thought*, New York, Bookman Associates, 1957, pp. 252–53; *cf*. C. M. Schirokauer, "Chu Hsi's Political Career: A Study in Ambivalence," in Wright and Twitchett, *op. cit.*, pp. 165–66.

76. "The Chou dynasty," *The Book of Lord Shang*, trans. J. J. L. Duyvendak, London, Probsthain, 1928, p. 228.

76. Story of hare, Fung Yu-lan, *A History of Chinese Philosophy*, Princeton, Princeton University Press, 1952, I, 317 (Han-fei-tzu, ch. 49).

76. "No gentleman," W. A. Rickett, *Kuan-tzu*, Hong Kong, Hong Kong University Press, 1965, p. 103 (VI, 16, 9a).

78. "Upheld," "Did not," "Sternest," "Without," B. Watson, *Records of the Grand Historian of China*, New York, Columbia University Press, 1961, II, 413, 419, 453, 462.

78. Eighteenth-century list, C. S. Gardner, *Chinese Traditional Historiography*, 2nd ed., Cambridge, Harvard University Press, 1961, pp. 100–104.

81. "The year," "The year," W. T. de Bary, *Sources of Chinese Tradition*, New York, Columbia University Press, 1960, p. 496.

82. "Official compilation," Lien-sheng Yang, "The Organization of Chinese Official Historiography: Principles and Methods of the Standard Histories from the T'ang through the Ming Dynasty," in Beasley and Pulleyblank, *op. cit.*, p. 53.

82. "The Diaries," W. Franke, "The Veritable Records of the Ming Dynasty (1368–1644)," in Beasley and Pulleyblank, *op. cit.*, p. 67.

83. "Among the different," *ibid.*, pp. 63, 64.

83. "Prescriptions," *ibid.*, p. 64.

84. "The Work," *ibid.*, p. 65.

85. "Two manuscript copies," *ibid.*, p. 73.

86. "I believe," *The Annals of Tacitus*, trans. D. R. Dudley, New York, New American Library, 1966, p. 128 (IV, 33); *cf*. M. L. W. Laistner, *The Greater Roman Historians*, Berkeley, University of California Press, 1947, pp. 113–14.

87. "I did not spare," *Alberuni's India*, London, Routledge & Kegan Paul, reprint Delhi, S. Chand & Co., 1964, p. 24.

87. "Everything," *ibid.*, p. 6.

87. "This book," *ibid.*, p. 7.

89. "The Grand Historian," B. Watson, *Ssu-ma Ch'ien: Grand Historian of China*, New York, Columbia University Press, 1958, pp. 49–50; *cf*. also de Bary, *Sources*.

90. "I have climbed," B. Watson, *Records of the Grand Historian*, II, 78.

91. "Even in more," Watson, *Ssu-ma Ch'ien*, p. 189.

91. "By nature," "Empress Lü," Watson, *Records*, I, 323.

92. "The Grand Historian," *ibid.*, p. 340.
92. "They always meant," J. Y. Liu, *The Chinese Knight-Errant*, London, Routledge & Kegan Paul, 1967, pp. 14–15.
92. "Men who stick," B. Watson, *Records*, II, 454.
94. "In contradiction," *The Literary Mind and the Carving of Dragons by Liu Hsieh*, trans. V. Yu-ching Shih, New York, Columbia University Press, 1959, p. 87 (modified).
94. "In all that," E. G. Pulleyblank, "Chinese Historical Criticism: Liu Chih-chi and Ssu-ma Kuang," in Beasley and Pulleyblank, *op. cit.*, p. 141.
96. "First note," *ibid.*, p. 162.
97. "Since I was young," D. S. Nivison, *The Life and Thought of Chang Hsüeh-ch'eng (1738–1801)*, Stanford, Stanford University Press, 1966, p. 35.
98. "One may therefore," *ibid.*, p. 145.
98. "When an extreme," *ibid.*, p. 159.
98. "There is for each," *ibid.*, p. 156.
99. "From emperors," Pulleyblank, "Chinese Historical Criticism," in Beasley and Pulleyblank, *op. cit.*, p. 144.
100. Watson, *Ssu-ma Ch'ien*, pp. 65–66.

4

Cosmographers: Time, Space, World, Great Ultimate

108. "If we apply," M. Sullivan, "The Heritage of Chinese Art," in R. Dawson, *The Legacy of China*, London, Oxford University Press, 1964, p. 195.
110. "We shall excel," J. Needham, "Time and Knowledge in China and the West," in J. T. Fraser, *The Voices of Time*, London, Allen Lane, the Penguin Press, 1968, pp. 126–27.
110. "The worthies," *ibid.*, p. 108.
111. "They determined," L. C. Goodrich, *A Short History of the Chinese People*, 3rd ed., New York, Harper & Row, 1959, p. 47.
112. "About four," J. Gernet, *Daily Life in China on the Eve of the Mongol Invasion 1250–1276*, London, Allen & Unwin, 1962, p. 182.
113. "At dawn," *ibid.*, pp. 187–88.
115. "For the Chinese," P. M. D'Elia, *Galileo in China: Relations through the Roman College between Galileo and the Jesuit Scientist-Missionaries (1610–1640)*, Cambridge, Harvard University Press, 1960, pp. 65–67, 77–78.
117. Trial of Jesuits, A. H. Rowbotham, *Missionary and Mandarin: The Jesuits at the Court of China*, Berkeley, University of California Press, 1942, ch. 6.
118. "The plumb-line," J. Needham, *Science and Civilisation in China*, London, Cambridge University Press, 1962, IV-1, p. 15 (*Hui Nan Tzu*, ch. 5).

118. "Magicians," *ibid.*, pp. 249–50.
118. "According," *ibid.*, p. 279.
119. "Does heaven," *The Complete Works of Chuang Tzu*, trans. B. Watson, New York, Columbia University Press, 1968, p. 154 (*Chuang Tzu*, ch. 14).
120. "Although Yin," A. Forke, *The World-Conception of the Chinese*, London, Probsthain, 1925, p. 203.
122. "Wood," W. T. de Bary, *Sources of Chinese Tradition*, New York, Columbia University Press, 1960, pp. 218–20.
122. "Heaven, earth," *ibid.*, p. 181.
123. "Collected," Fung Yu-lan, *A History of Chinese Philosophy*, Princeton, Princeton University Press, 1953, II, 21–22.
123. "Within," *ibid.*, p. 20.
123. "Wood," *ibid.*, pp. 20–21.
124. "The Non-ultimate," W.-T. Chan, *A Source Book in Chinese Philosophy*, Princeton, Princeton University Press, 1963, p. 463.
125. "Heaven is like," de Bary, *op. cit.*, p. 210.
125. "If today," Chan, *op. cit.*, p. 642.
126. "The seeds," *The Complete Works of Chuang Tzu*, pp. 195–96 (*Chuang Tzu*, ch. 18).
126. "When heaven," Fung Yu-lan, *op. cit.*, p. 152.
127. "The Great Ultimate," Chan, *op. cit.*, p. 640.
127. "Those who," *Reflections on Things at Hand: The Neo-Confucian Anthology Compiled by Chu Hsi and Lü Tsu-ch'ien*, trans. W.-T. Chan, New York, Columbia University Press, 1967, p. 15.

5

Philosophers: Forms of Language and Thought

131. "It is," Ping-ti Ho and Tang Tsou, *China in Crisis*, Chicago, University of Chicago Press, 1968, I, 81.
132. "Too complex," A. C. Graham, "The Place of Reason in the Chinese Philosophical Tradition," in R. Dawson, *The Legacy of China*, London, Oxford University Press, 1964, pp. 54–55.
132. "It seems likely," *ibid.*, p. 55.
136. "Nothing but," A. A. Bennett, *John Fryer: The Introduction of Western Science and Technology into Nineteenth-Century China*, Harvard East Asian Monographs No. 24, Cambridge, Harvard University Press, 1967, p. 26.
137. "We must carefully," *ibid.*, p. 31.
137. A. Forke, in H. Gipper, *Bausteine zur Sprachinhaltsforschung*, Düsseldorf, 1963, pp. 215–79.
138. "From this," Chang Tung-sun, "A Chinese Philosopher's Theory of Knowledge," *ETC*, Spring, 1952, p. 215 (trans.

by Li An-che, first in the *Yenching Journal of Social Studies*, Vol. I, No. 2, Peking, 1939).

138.   "In putting," *ibid.*, p. 220.

138.   Margouliès, H. Gipper, *op. cit.*

139.   "Like the logic," *op. cit.* (originally *Anthropological Linguistics*, I, 1959).

140.   "The inhibiting," J. Needham, "Poverties and Triumphs of the Chinese Scientific Tradition," in A. C. Crombie, *Scientific Change*, London, Heinemann, 1963.

142.   Magical aura of Chinese writing, J. Gernet, "La Chine, aspects et fonctions psychologiques de l'écriture," in *L'Ecriture et la psychologie des peuples*, Centre International de Synthèse, XXIIe Semaine de Synthèse, Paris, Armand Colin, 1963.

143.   "*Wen*, or pattern," *The Literary Mind and the Carving of Dragons by Liu Hsieh*, trans. V. Yu-ching Shih, New York, Columbia University Press, 1959, pp. 8–9.

144.   "Some one asked," *Reflections on Things at Hand: The Neo-Confucian Anthology Compiled by Chu-Hsi and Lü Tsu-ch'ien*, trans. Wing-tsit Chan, New York, Columbia University Press, 1967, p. 22.

144.   "It will be found," A. C. Graham, *Two Chinese Philosophers*, London, Lund Humphries, 1958, p. 8.

145.   "That by which," *ibid.*, p. 8.

145.   "That a tree flowers," *ibid.*, p. 90.

145.   "How do you," *ibid.*, p. 12.

145.   "Fundamentally," Wing-tsit Chan, *A Source Book in Chinese Philosophy*, Princeton, Princeton University Press, 1963, p. 634; my capitalization.

146.   "Our original nature," *Reflections on Things at Hand*, p. 54 (my capitalization).

146.   "If one's moral," *ibid.*, p. 74.

147.   "The operation," *ibid.*, p. 75.

148.   "Since the Buddhist," *ibid.*, pp. 287–88.

148.   "Buddhism," A. C. Graham, *op. cit.*, p. 86.

148.   "They differ," *Reflections on Things at Hand*, p. 282.

149.   "The Zen doctrine," A. C. Graham, *op. cit.*, p. 86.

149.   Knowledge-action, D. S. Nivison, "The Problem of 'Knowledge' and 'Action' in Chinese Thought since Wang Yang-ming," in A. F. Wright, *Studies in Chinese Thought*, Chicago, University of Chicago Press, 1953.

149.   "The reason," *Instructions for Practical Living and Other Neo-Confucian Writings by Wang Yang-ming*, trans. Wing-tsit Chan, New York, Columbia University Press, 1963, p. 19.

150.   "Knowledge in its genuine," *ibid.*, p. 93.

150.   "Suppose," *ibid.*, pp. 10–11.

151.   "Generally speaking," *ibid.*, p. 183.

152.   "When his mind," *ibid.*, p. 273.

152. "Buddhism claims," *ibid.*, p. 105.
153. "The great man," *ibid.*, p. 272.
153. "The doctrine," J. Dewey, *Democracy and Education*, New York, Macmillan, 1916, p. 393.
153. "To learn archery," *Instructions for Practical Living*, p. 100.
154. "To call anything," Dewey, *op. cit.*, p. 393.
154. "To be earnest," *Instructions*, p. 100.
154. "What the word," Dewey, *op. cit.*, p. 207.
154. "In learning," *Instructions*, p. 100.
154. "The general features," Dewey, p. 176.
155. Puritanism, W. Eberhard, *Guilt and Sin in Traditional China*, Berkeley, University of California Press, 1967.
156. "I hear," L. C. Goodrich, *The Literary Inquisition of Ch'ien-lung*, Baltimore, American Council of Learned Societies, Waverly Press, 1935, pp. 89–90.
156. "Although censorable," *ibid.*, p. 39.
157. "In case," *ibid.*, p. 40.
157. "It was a brave," *ibid.*, p. 42.
157. "Enclose boundless space," A. Fang, "Rhymeprose on Literature: The Wên-fu of Lu Chi (A.D. 261–303)," in J. L. Bishop, *Studies in Chinese Literature*, Harvard-Yenching University Studies XXI, Cambridge, Harvard University Press, 1965, p. 10.
159. "There is joy," *ibid.*, p. 10.

INDEX

Machiavelli, Niccolò, 91
Ma Ho-chih, 55
Male and female forces, 43, 109, 119, 120
Manchus, 59
Mann, Thomas, 63–64
Margoliès, Georges, 137–138
Marriages, 5–6
Mathematics, 21, 115, 116, 139
Matter-Energy (*ch'i*), 144, 145–146, 148
Ma Tuan-lin, 96–97
"Mean" people, social hierarchy and, 10, 11
Medicine, 21
Medieval clocks, 110
Medieval philosophy, 146
Mencius, 156
Mercury poisoning, 43
Metal (element), 109, 121–122, 124, 146
Mi Fei, 37, 52, 54, 57, 61
Ming Dynasty: historiography during, 82, 84–85; individualism in painting during, 58–59
Missionaries, astronomy and, 114–117
Mo Yu-jen, 44
Mohammedan astronomy, 115–116
Monet, Claude, 37
Montaigne, Michel de, 151
Months, timekeeping and, 111
Moslem astronomy, 114
Moslem historians, Chinese historians compared with, 87–88
Mothers, 5–6
Mo Ti, 110–111
Mustard Seed Garden Painting Manual, 56, 57

Nanking, 115
Nan-t'ien, 37
Narratives from the States (Tso), 100
Nature: landscape painting and, 38–40; pattern in, 143; realistic painting of, 35–36; scholars' sensitivity to, 25

Navigation, ship, 118
Needham, Joseph, 139–140
Neo-Confucianism: attack on Buddhism by, 147–148, 155; calligraphy and, 50–52; founder of, 123; historical writing and, 74; *li* (principle) in, 145; puritanism in, 155; view of art in, 50
Nero, 92
New History of T'ang, 73
New Year celebration, 113, 114
Ni Tsan, 53–54, 55, 63
Northern tradition in painting, 54
Novels: dissipation and writing of, 59; historical borrowings in, 68–69; puritanism in, 155

Officials: biographies of, 70–74; examination system and, 15–22; in social hierarchy, 10–11; time observation by, 107, 112
Organic development doctrines, 153
Ou-yang Chiung, 37
Ou-yang Hsiu, 97

Painting, 27–64; amateurs in, 47–50; analytical exercises and musical analogies in, 55–57; connoisseurship in, 22–26; craftsmen in, 47–50; detachment in, 63–64; forgery in, 57–58; history and, 67–69; individualism in, 59–62; *i* style of, 41–42; landscape, 38–40; life-breath in, 35–37; pattern in, 142–143; professionals in, 47–50; puritanism in, 155; range of subjects in, 29–30; realism in, 67–68; sadness in, 63; search for inspiration and longevity in, 42–45; spontaneity in, 40–42, 49; techniques in, 30–31; temporal quality of, 107–108; Tung's radical conservatism in, 54–55
Pa-ta Shan-jên, 61
Pattern, 142–144
Paul, Dr., 116
P'ei K'ai, 33
P'ei Min, General, 42–43

Peking, 115
Pendulum clocks, 110
P'eng (legendary bird), 64
Pharmacology, 109
Philosophy, 129–159; expressions for existence and, 135–136; high esteem of, 16, 21; history and, 88; Neo-Confuscian attack on Buddhism and, 147–148; puritanism and censorship and, 155–157; time and space in, 108
Pictographs, 133
Plato, 127, 137, 146
Plutarch, 85–86
Po Chü-i, 46–47
Poetry: antithesis in, 144; detachment in, 63; drinking and, 43–47; examination system and, 18, 19; history and, 68; superiority of Chinese language for, 135
Political values, 8–10
Polybius, 87
Population: breakdown of examination system and increase in, 22; number of, 3
Pragmatists, 97
Presocratic philosophers, 145
Principle (*li*), 144–146, 148
Propriety (principle), 146
Proverbs, 5, 6, 7, 25
Puritanism, 155–157

Radical conservatism in painting, 54–55
Radicals (language), 133, 137
Realism: inner force and moral aim of art and, 36–37; in painting, 31, 67–68
Records of the Historian (Ssu-ma), 69, 70, 77–78
Renaissance, 29
Ricci, Matthew, 16, 21–22, 116
Righteousness (principle), 146
Roman historians, Chinese historians compared with, 86–87

Sadness in painting, 63
Schall, Adam, 117

Scholars: biographies of, 70–74; connoisseurship and, 22–26; family prestige and, 5; individualistic styles and, 58–59; path of life of, 107; social class of, 11; soldiers and, 16
Schools, 12–14
Science, language and development of, 140
Science and Civilization in China (Needham), 139
Seasons, Five Elements and, 121
Sexual forces, 119
Sexual techniques to lengthen life, 43
Shang Dynasty, 76
Shen Fu, 24
Shih-ch'i, 61–62
Shih K'o, 41
Shih-t'ao, 59–60, 61, 76
Ship navigation, 118
Shun, Emperor, 76
Social evolution, 126
Social hierarchy, 10–11
Socrates, 149
Soldiers, standing of, 16
Sophists, 108
"Sorrow of Standing Alone, The" (Han), 100
Southern tradition in painting, 54
Spontaneity, calligraphy and, 50; childhood and, 107; painting and, 40–42, 49
Ssu-ma Ch'ien, 69, 70, 77–78, 89–94, 95, 97, 100–101, 158
Ssu-ma Kuang, 95–96
Ssu-ma T'an, 89–90
Stability of culture, 4
Standard Histories, 80, 82
Stoicism: history and, 88; idea of universe in, 127; poetry and, 63
Styles of painting, 30, 41
Suicides, filial piety and, 7–8
Sundials, 110, 111
Sung Ch'i, 97
Sung Dynasty: institutional history of, 96; painting in, 48
Sung Jo-ssu, 73